Gender Planning in Development Agencies

Meeting the Challenge

A report of a workshop held
at The Cherwell Centre, Oxford, England
in May 1993

Edited by Mandy Macdonald

Oxfam
UK and Ireland

© Oxfam (UK and Ireland) 1994

A catalogue record for this book is available from the British Library

ISBN 0 85598 262 4 Hardback
ISBN 0 85598 263 2 Paperback

Published by Oxfam (UK and Ireland)
274 Banbury Road, Oxford OX2 7DZ
(Oxfam is registered as a charity, No. 202918)

Designed and typeset by Oxfam Design Department OX/583/93
Printed by Oxfam Print Unit

Typeset in Palatino
Cover PMS 212
Printed on environment–friendly paper

Contents

2

Section III: Thematic papers

Section IV: Case studies

Acknowledgements

Thanks are due to everyone who helped to organise the EUROSTEP workshop which took place in Oxford in May 1993, and to all those who helped to produce this report.

The core group which planned and coordinated the workshop consisted of Brita Nielsen, EUROSTEP secretariat; Diana Vinding, IBIS; Anna Foca, MOLISV; and Eugenia Piza-López, Oxfam (UK and Ireland). Many people within Oxfam helped to host the event. Twenty-five individuals and agencies (listed in Appendix 3) contributed their ideas and experience. Mandy Macdonald recorded the proceedings of the workshop, and produced the report.

The following agencies sponsored the production of this book: ActionAid, HIVOS, IBIS, Mani Tese, MS, NCOS, NOVIB, and Oxfam (UK and Ireland).

Foreword

Eugenia Piza-López
Coordinator, Gender and Development Unit, Oxfam (UK and Ireland)

In 1975 the United Nations declared the International Decade for Women. This initiative prompted debate, research, analysis, and movement-building, and boosted the work of activists worldwide. It legitimised women's claims for equality and social change at all levels from the state to the household, from the public domain to the private sphere.

So why is it that we women of European non-governmental development organisations (NGDOs) found ourselves meeting, nearly twenty years on, to discuss and agree strategies for advancing this agenda? The answer is simple: we still have a long way to go before the goals of the Forward-Looking Strategies, stated by over 5,000 women of many nations at Nairobi in 1985, are achieved.

However, many years of action have taught us a great deal. We have learnt about strategies to promote institutional change; where the blockages lie; how to operate within and outside the system; and the importance of building institutional alliances with men and women working towards the same objectives inside and outside our organisations.

We have also learned about the multiple realities and profound differences between women; about the multi-faceted nature of women's identity and oppression; about how women work through their differences in order to build alliances and new forms of social organisation; about the discrepancies and differences which can and do divide women individually and collectively.

We have learned — and are still learning — about the possibilities for women from the North and the South to work together, with common agendas but different roles, and the challenges which this relationship presents. From academics, development workers, and our own practice we have developed a holistic understanding of gender issues and how they interrelate with development at both local and global levels.

A major objective of the workshop on which this book is based was to share this knowledge and identify points of similarity and difference between our various experiences. The issues we are concerned about are not marginal to the development debate. Gender is not a question of securing a small slice of the cake for women in development projects. Our proposals have profound implications for the way in which development agencies work and the way in which development issues are conceptualised and approached. Gender issues are not secondary or of 'special interest', but are central to sustainable development. Women's views are not the views of a 'special interest' group. Women represent half the world's population, and their perspectives are a major component of development.

Gender and development practitioners are saying that perceived divisions and hierarchies between 'development' and 'gender' issues (with the latter somehow secondary to the former) must be challenged and broken down. Mainstreaming gender is about introducing women's perspectives into all areas of development work and claiming both the private and the public domains, individual and collective experience, as legitimate spheres for development action.

The workshop held in Oxford in May 1993 was the beginning of a process aimed at gaining a collective understanding of what, as gender and development practitioners, we are proposing, and how we would like to move forward. The specific objectives that gathered the EUROSTEP agencies together were:

• to promote an exchange of experiences in research, monitoring, and evaluation, and information about practical tools and strategies for future work;

• to promote the development of new methodologies and systematise best practice;

- to strengthen member agencies' work on gender and to identify ways of working together to avoid duplication, move forward effectively, and meet forthcoming challenges.

For Oxfam UK/Ireland, as the host agency, the workshop was a valuable exercise in coordination and an important opportunity to learn from all the EUROSTEP agencies and share our experiences, difficulties, and achievements. There are many reasons why this meeting was particularly important. As development agencies we need to adapt to new realities and challenges, including those posed by the women's movements, which demand a rethinking and reappraisal of Northern agencies' role in promoting women's and gender-sensitive development. We need to enhance our understanding of how we can play a more active and coordinated role in strengthening Southern women's movements so that they can continue challenging discrimination and marginalisation on the grounds of gender. We need to work collectively towards improving the quality of international cooperation for women, particularly women in poorer and marginal communities with whom we work. And we need to define common strategies to influence the direction of multilateral and bilateral aid, which has a decisive impact on Southern women's livelihoods and well-being.

During the meeting we became clearly aware of the need to address these issues and to systematise our experience so as to share the lessons learned with NGOs, groups, and organisations in the North and the South. The creation of the EUROSTEP gender network is the beginning of this process. We are now consolidating our first steps. We will be working together in a structured process, looking at ways of influencing the policies of the European Community and preparing the ground for the International Conference on Population and Development (Cairo, 1994) and the UN Conference on Women (Beijing, 1995).

In this work, Oxfam (UK and Ireland) will be the lead agency on gender and development lobbying, and NCOS will lead on programme learning. Together with a steering group, we are already preparing a two-year lobbying and learning programme and planning a future meeting in Denmark, to be hosted by MS.

The future holds exciting prospects and the development of new ways of working. Together we will have to address critical issues and face important challenges. As gender and development professionals, we will have to overcome obstacles in our own institutions, while maintaining a positive and hopeful spirit. We will have to work, within the institutional framework, on our own roles, workloads, and decision-making capacities, and particularly to address the lack of control over resources that hinders many gender specialists.

Instruments will need to be developed to evaluate and monitor progress and the impact of EUROSTEP agencies' work from a gender-based perspective, both at the 'macro' level of policy and in our everyday work at the 'micro' level of projects. Mechanisms must be sought to overcome institutional differences between the agencies: differences in policy, different ways of working, different structures in order to create sustainable alliances.

We will need a dynamic analysis of gender issues which reflects the concerns and realities of the women we are working with in the South. And finally, we will have to clarify our role as Northern agencies *vis à vis* Southern women's movements and organisations, striving to appreciate and embrace in our thinking and action the full complexities of North–South cooperation.

Oxford, November 1993

Opening speech

Audrey Moser, Trustee of Oxfam (UK and Ireland)

First of all, I want to offer a warm welcome to you all on behalf of Oxfam. You have come here from many countries and many different backgrounds, and with a great wealth of varied experience to contribute. I'm particularly pleased to be here, because of my own experience and interest in international NGOs: I worked in two such agencies, based in Geneva, from 1955 to 1986. Since my background is in work with children, I have inevitably found myself working with, and in contact with, women from many different countries. So it is a privilege to be here with colleagues from different countries to open this workshop today.

I bring you good wishes also from the Chair of Oxfam (UK/I), Mary Cherry, and the Director, David Bryer, both of whom regret that they cannot be with us today.

Oxfam (UK/I) is delighted to host this meeting, given its commitment to gender and its concern to influence the development agenda on this issue. The meeting takes place at an important time in Oxfam's history: its fiftieth anniversary coincides with a significant shift in attitudes towards gender issues. Oxfam has put gender firmly on its agenda as a strategic objective for the institution in its development and humanitarian work overseas and its advocacy, education, and campaigning work in the UK and Ireland.

Since 1985, when it was created, the Gender and Development Unit (GADU) has done much work in training, publications, research, education, and advocacy. Now, I am glad to say, Oxfam has agreed on a corporate policy on gender and development, and this was approved and endorsed by the Executive Council on 16 May 1993. This represents a significant endorsement of the work of GADU.

As a result of this policy, we can now see more clearly the immense task ahead and get a clearer view of how we can move forward to achieve our objectives in our overseas programme, in our work in the UK and Ireland, and in management. I would emphasise that last element — management — because, as we all know, the battle to achieve gender-awareness in our own institutions is by no means over yet, either in the UK and Ireland or, I imagine, in other European countries.

One important part of our strategy will be to assist in strengthening the lobby of bilateral and multilateral agencies on gender issues and promoting advocacy work together with networks and organisations both in the North and the South, including institutional support for international gender-focused lobbying networks. Many international agencies now recognise that gender is a crucial issue to consider in the construction of democratic, participatory, and sustainable development processes. And this recognition is taking place at a moment of important changes in the world order.

The present social and economic crisis has had devastating effects on the poor of the South, and these have been particularly bad for women. Cuts in public expenditure, coupled with discriminatory employment practices, have increased female unemployment and led to poorer labour conditions for women. Falling commodity prices have forced farmers into more intense cash-cropping, creating more manual work for women without any corresponding increase in what they are paid. Structural adjustment policies, particularly cuts in state subsidies on drinking water, food, health, eduction, and transport, have had a disproportionate effect on women.

Widespread armed and ethnic conflict also has a particular impact on women. Women and their children form the majority of refugee or displaced populations, and the proportion of woman-maintained households in turbulent situations has grown. In addition, women in situations of conflict suffer abuses, such as sexual assault or exploitation, which are not experienced by men.

Environmental destruction has a multiple and growing impact on women. Increasingly they cannot provide fuel, wood, and water for their families' needs. Urbanisation has cut women off from traditional support systems. Industrialisation exposes women to hazardous substances and dangerous processes in factories with poor safety regulations. In many areas of the world, the spread of AIDS is particularly affecting women as sufferers and as carers.

Governments, multilateral agencies, and NGOs do not always understand the different impact of development aid on women and men, and this has led in many cases to a further marginalisation of women from traditional decision-making structures. It has displaced them from their economic activities and has meant that their valuable knowledge and their potential contribution to development has been ignored. Development aid is less effective when women are not participating on an equal footing.

The challenges for EUROSTEP agencies and individuals committed to working on gender and development are greater than ever. Promoting a gender-based perspective leads development practitioners to look for alternatives which will promote women's rights to self-determination, choice, and more equitable relations in general. And that means radical transformations at all levels, from the household to the state. EUROSTEP agencies are in a privileged position to contribute to those changes, with our commitment and closeness to the needs and perspectives of poor women, our role in North/South solidarity, and our focus on advocacy.

This meeting is an important contribution to the process of widening understanding of gender, both in Oxfam and all EUROSTEP member agencies. EUROSTEP is providing the space and the opportunity to bring together skills, knowledge, and a vast range of experience which will undoubtedly take the debate forward. We hope that this workshop will provide the inspiration and impetus needed to meet these many challenges and will strengthen the links between practitioners for joint action and support.

It is with pleasure, therefore, that I declare this workshop open, and wish you very successful and fruitful work together.

Issues arising
from the workshop

Mandy Macdonald

1

Introduction

What do we mean by gender?

Since the mid-1980s, there has been a gradual shift in thinking among feminist academics and development professionals about women and men in the development process. Previous women and development (WAD) or women in development (WID) approaches have focused on analysing the roles, rights, and responsibilities *specifically* of women in the effort to correct their exclusion from and invisibility (and silence) in development planning. But WID tended to see women in isolation, so in many cases it looked for solutions that were not holistic, resulting often in women's interests being addressed by women's components in larger programmes and projects which were largely within 'traditional' approaches, supporting women in their traditional roles without necessarily questioning the sexual division of labour. This approach also did not aim to change men. The gender and development (or GAD) approach, theoretically at least, foregrounds the *interdependent* character of women's and men's positions in society, referring to the culturally determined roles which women and men take on or are assigned in different societies, i.e. the sexual division of labour.

Gender and development considers women's condition of economic inequality, and their status *vis à vis* men in the same cultural strata; it also considers men, collectively and individually, but it focuses especially on women because of discrimination against women. However, GAD does not assume that all women everywhere are the same and have the same problems: a GAD analysis attempts to incorporate questions of class, caste, and ethnicity into a gender-based perspective.

In a large forestry project in South India, the objective is to regenerate the forest for sustainable commercial use, providing livelihoods for local communities. This includes various stages of the production and commercialisation cycle: planting, harvesting, marketing. All these inputs are directed at men. A WID approach to meeting women's needs in this project might be to develop, at a later stage, a specific project for women such as jam-making. A GAD approach, on the other hand, would be more integrated from the earliest planning stages of the project. It would consider women's productive roles and try to integrate women into the production process on an equal footing; it would identify the obstacles to women's participation and try to overcome them; it would look for ways to break down resistance from men. It would thus seek more structural change in the balance of power between women and men.

But this change in focus does not mean either that women have abandoned the struggle, or that gender equality has been achieved. GAD looks at relations of power between women and men, and a basic assumption when we consider such relations is that they are concerned with power, and that men and women start from unequal positions. Integrating gender into the mainstream of development (mainstreaming gender) continues to mean improving the position of women, that is, questioning and working towards redefining the sexual division of labour, and involving men in that redefinition. This has implications for development policy, programme and project design, appraisal, implementation, monitoring, and evaluation. And it calls for change within the institutional structures and cultures of development NGOs (NGDOs) themselves.

In practice, NGDOs in the North and the South are coping slowly and unevenly with these conceptual shifts. The distinction between WID and GAD is subtle and complex, and also expensive to implement in terms of financial and human resources. Gender may perhaps appear to be no more than verbal fencing to an overworked and underfunded development worker in a poor rural community, for whom an income-generating project for women based on a traditionally feminine activity such as cooking or sewing may seem the only strategy for giving women access to money and the space to organise. Many NGDOs continue to do their work with women uncritically. Others are struggling with new analyses, new policies, rethinking their own institutions in the light of the prescriptions they have been making for Southern partners. There is also a new recognition of the fact that Northern NGOs reflect the context and culture of their own societies and therefore contain the contradictions of those societies. In both Northern and Southern NGOs, women are not a monolithic block but a varied and dynamic group containing its own differences and contradictions.

Nothing is gender-neutral

'... all projects, whatever their technical nature, have a gender dimension by always targeting men, women, or both. This implies that, regardless of whether we are dealing with a men's or a women's project, it will always impinge upon the opposite gender. All women's projects will affect the men's position, and *vice versa*. Hence no project can claim gender neutrality.'

(Cathrine Hasse, 'Target Group, Gender and Visibility in Ibis Projects', report for Ibis, Copenhagen, July 1992)

Whose development is it anyway?

Gender is a political issue, because it is about power. It is a political issue also because it seeks to bring the private sphere into the public arena of debate and action. What happens in development, and how seriously gender is taken on board both in overseas programmes and within institutions' Northern headquarters, depends on relationships of power which are all too often vertical: relations between North and South, management and staff, men and women. Who defines and sets agendas in development cooperation? Who takes policy decisions? Who holds the purse-strings? To a large extent, working from a gender and development point of view means working to change the balance of power in those processes at many levels, from the household to the international institution.

Development aid itself is a political issue. It reflects the interests of donors; and many NGDOs, while trying to challenge existing power-relations institutionally, nonetheless have subtle ways of directing the aid process. Recent research (for instance, Ann Lotherington's) has shown that the personal outlook and preferences of project officers in the North have a much greater influence on shaping projects in the South than have been generally recognised. Aid donors give aid on the basis of their ideas of what constitutes development, which spring not only from their own ideologies and system of values, but from their prejudices and fears. This can happen even in institutions devoted to combating poverty and unfair distribution of resources of all kinds. It can also happen with regard to gender, where the North is in many cases imposing its understanding of gender on the South. It is thus not surprising that project partners become adept at proposing projects according to what they think or know aid donors want to hear.

A key idea underlying this report is that Northern NGDOs must put their own houses in order with regard to gender if they are to improve the quality of their development cooperation by taking gender seriously into account overseas. This means looking at the inequalities in the way donor agencies run their organisations and manage overseas programmes and projects. It means finding ways of working with the contradictions in both North and South, ways of working within a recognition of North/South power structures, and mechanisms that will enable us to do this. We cannot pretend that this is easy to do. Over and over again, efforts to mainstream gender in our organisations meet with lip-service, tokenism, avoidance, inertia, ridicule or outright hostility. Chapters 2 and 3 of this section examine in more detail this process of transforming gender-relations in our institutions.

Strategies of resistance and avoidance

As Naila Kabeer reminds us, many development planners 'have successfully resisted learning from increasing numbers of non-governmental or political organisations which have made women's empowerment and men's conscientisation their primary objectives' ('Gender, development and training: raising awareness in development planning' (Bangalore, 1990; see GADU Newspack 14). Resistance can come from all three points of the development cooperation triangle: from within Northern institutions, from Southern partner NGOs, and from men and women in target groups. Resistance can be passive (avoidance; failing to act on policy or allocate resources; invoking gender-neutrality) or active (invoking culture as sacrosanct; accusations of Western — or feminist — imperialism). Many NGDOs have found that while challenging or changing class-based or race-based inequalities is treated as a legitimate primary objective of development, attempts to change gender-based inequalities can be seen as unwarranted interference in another culture. Within our own institutions, gender tends to be ranked below or subsumed into other areas of concern. Even where agencies have a successful equal-opportunities policy in terms of employment, recognition of gender-based differences tends to disappear once staff are in post: the multiple roles and responsibilities of women employees are not recognised, but neither are they treated equally with men in terms of promotion and access to decision-making.

> '... Planning for the needs of low-income women is not necessarily "feminist" in content. Indeed, the vast majority of policies, programs and projects directed at women worldwide are concerned with women *within* their engendered position in the sexual division of labour ... Practical gender needs only become "feminist" in content if and when they are transformed into strategic gender needs.'
>
> (Caroline Moser, 'Gender planning in the Third World: meeting practical and strategic gender needs', *World Development* 17/11 (1989), p. 1804)

To what extent do Northern NGDOs have the right to try to change gender relations in Southern countries? Where, when, and by what means are they justified in trying to do so? One answer to these questions is that they cannot avoid having an influence. They already change gender (and other) relations by their very presence, by the choices they make as to whom they assist, by the way they guide or advise partner NGOs to design their projects and draw up their project proposals. All aid is conditioned all the time, by virtue of the unequal relations between North and South. Views are shaped and choices conditioned, too, by the identity of the protagonists in aid relationships. Northern NGDOs need to recognise that they do not always talk to the whole spectrum of people involved in a project or programme: they may talk mainly to men of a certain class, or to women who are not feminist. To achieve a gender-based perspective, then, agencies need to make sure that they talk and listen to women.

Another answer can be found by listening to women from the culture involved. If they identify their own culture's areas of oppression and injustice and request the help of Northern NGDOs in redressing injustices, women in donor NGDOs are in a stronger position to defend and promote what women themselves have identified as their gender-determined interests. At the same time, agencies must be aware that these interests are not a monolithic block, but that there are divisions and differences, even hostilities, between women in the South, as in the North. To poor indigenous women in a rural village in Guatemala, a middle-class white woman from a national NGO, fluent in Spanish and English but probably not in Mam or Kekchí, may seem every bit as alien as a male manager on a flying visit from Oxfam or NCOS. And the women from the national NGO, members of a tiny minority in their country to have achieved a professional career, may not automatically intuit the particular gender-determined needs or interests of the poor rural women. Gender-awareness needs to be promoted at every stage of a project and at every level of all institutions involved.

Chapters 5 and 6 in this section address various aspects of these questions and try to suggest some answers.

What about men?

'A gender analysis which focuses on women alone is incomplete. If gender is about relations between men and women, then the male side of the equation must also be figured in. If women's gender identities are to be changed, then men's must change also.'

(Sarah White, 'Making men an issue: gender planning for "the other half"', Keynote Paper 3)

Just as gender is a political issue, so the private sphere is a political arena. Households are sites of power-relations like any other institution. Indeed the family-based household is a primary site of gender-determined relations, and the balance of those relations is no more sacrosanct because they are based principally if not exclusively on gender-differences than on any other power balance.

Everything women do and everything we do as NGDOs, every project we design and plan with women, is done with one eye on women's domestic roles and tasks. But men are part of the family too; and development planning for and with men rarely puts men's roles in the private sphere into the calculations. Has the time come to put men back into the gender equation? Does mainstreaming imply that men now have to be involved, sensitised, trained, and challenged, expected to take their part in changing the balance of power in gender relations?

This is an extremely vexed question. If gender is about women **and** men, it is logical to assume that the gender-based balance of power cannot be changed by women alone. Indeed, one of the lessons of many years of WID work is that it is possible to increase women's access to income generation, decision-making, community leadership, and so on, but that if men do not change their behaviour, particularly if they refuse to share responsibility in the household, women are in the end faced with impossible choices between their triple roles as carers, producers, and community members.

But will bringing men back into the equation, while men still have so much power, simply divert attention away again from women? Men see that they may have a lot of entrenched power to lose by just entering into dialogue on gender roles and relations. The Danish NGDO MS found, at a participatory rural appraisal workshop in Kenya where participants were divided into single-sex groups to identify needs and interests, that the women were very active, full of discussion and ideas, while the men were anxious and expressed not their own interests but their fear of what they might lose through the women's interests being served. The men were unable to articulate their own interests, because they had never had to. Their interests were served, by default, by any activity that was not specifically earmarked for women. Men's interests in most cases lie simply in maintaining the *status quo* as regards gender, and they see their position as needing no negotiation, because it is backed up by culture and tradition.

'Gender planning for the other half' is thus a process that is necessary but fraught with pitfalls, if women's advances in changing the balance of power are not to be endangered. Men have to be brought into the process; they have to be willing to change; but there must also be recognition that women's struggle is their own struggle and is not to be taken over by men. There is a delicate balance between making men's roles and interests 'visible' again and letting their reassert their dominance. What are the mechanisms to ensure that supposedly gender-neutral projects do not become men's projects by default? We do still have to give attention to women's own space, the need for women to develop in their own terms; and it is important to work at all levels; from the grassroots or micro-level, where women's space is most negotiable, to the international or macro-level, the level of policy and legislation, where it is arguably least negotiable.

On the other hand, it is arguable that the problem will never be solved until men are brought into the task of solving it. Some NGDOs are now beginning to consider using male gender trainers, and mixed partner organisations are being encouraged to develop gender policies and to look at the roots of structural gender-based inequalities, domestic violence, and the like.

Incorporating gender into all aspects of NGDO policy and practice does require and lead to a more complex analysis of development; but it is a truer, fairer, and more rewarding one.

Papers relevant to this chapter

'An ABC of institutionalising gender' by Georgina Ashworth (Keynote Paper 1)

'Gender-aware policy and planning: a social-relations perspective' by Naila Kabeer (Keynote Paper 2)

'Making men an issue: gender planning for the "other half"' by Sarah White (Keynote Paper 3)

2

Policy

'In order for donor organisations to be credible, they must have a gender policy that reflects a commitment to gender equity within their own organisations as well as overseas.'

(Workshop participant)

A development agency's gender policy, besides underpinning and defining its practice, forms the link between internal institutional issues (who makes policy? how does gender policy rank with the organisation's other policies? is it top-down, or participatory?) and external programme issues (the agency's relations with project partners, the balance of power between donor, partners, and grass-roots groups, the nature of consultation, and the interlocutors involved). These are political, not technical issues, determining the agency's credibility and its qualification to administer aid. Moreover, a gender policy must be not just a body of ideas informally accepted by sympathetic people in an organisation, but a written document, which can be invoked as a standard for measuring practice and used as a basis for discussing gender with partner organisations.

The establishment of a clear gender policy has repercussions beyond our own projects. Northern agencies can help to strengthen the women's lobby in the South via their gender policies: for instance, by supporting women's autonomous organisations, which can be a useful channel for promoting changes in gender relations in other, non-gender-specific projects.

This section ends with a checklist of recommendations for agencies engaged in developing a gender policy, with reference both to the institution's internal practice and to the policy it devises in relation to its overseas programmes.

Some NGDO experiences

Different agencies are at very different stages in the development of their gender policies, and continued sharing of ideas and experiences is crucial in order to assist policy development in those agencies recently embarking on mainstreaming gender. For those agencies which do have an established, accepted policy on gender, the issue is more often one of getting the policy translated into practice, both within the institution itself and in overseas programmes. In every case, the creation of a properly elaborated policy on women or gender has been due to the presence and activity of WID or GAD staff in the institution and women in partner organisations.

The experience of HIVOS in developing a gender policy is recounted in Case Study 1. Here, more briefly, are some experiences of other NGDOs.

Oxfam (UK/I) had its policy on gender finally approved in May 1993, after six years of preparation, debate, and negotiation, and twelve previous drafts of the policy document. Oxfam learned valuable lessons from the equal-opportunity process, and had clearly benefited from having a specific gender and development unit, GADU (*see* Case Study 3). GADU's gender policy was approved at a time of backlash, in a context where women are losing ground in development agencies as well as in society at large. Many equal-opportunities struggles have to be revived. The existence of a gender policy in itself is only a beginning: what is most important is how the policy is integrated into the organisation's instruments (budget lines, project criteria) and operational tools (manuals and guidelines) and into day-to-day practice within the organisation's culture and ideology. If management is committed to gender on paper only, nothing will be achieved. Here there are gaps in management structures in Oxfam: the specialist units, of which GADU is one, are advisory only and do not have a decision-making role.

ACORD, a European consortium of agencies, is in the process of becoming a gender-positive organisation, taking a proactive role towards work on gender issues, and not simply a gender-accepting one, where gender issues are merely recognised. It has formulated and debated a gender policy, growing out of the existing WID policy; but while this is in general a positive development, there has been one ironic result: the production of a gender policy led to the disappearance of a specific forum for women in ACORD.

MS (Denmark) has an official policy document on women and development: *Half and Half: Guidelines for Development Cooperation with Women*, which was published in early 1993 after three years of work by people in MS, both in Denmark and in the South. However, MS has found that difficulties arise at the point of implementation. A chief problem is simply resistance from men or from structures that preserve male power. MS found it necessary to use both male and female staff to promote the gender policy and to train partners and programme officers in gender issues, and to have structures and personnel such as a gender consultant close to management to ensure implementation. Ongoing monitoring and the promotion of a permanent dialogue on gender in the organisation are strategies for keeping gender on the agenda. (See Case Study 4.)

Novib (Netherlands) has chosen women as one of its three priority themes or lines of action (see Case Study 7) and its gender policy is extensively set out in a strategic policy document, *Contours for Novib's policy concerning women: work-plan 1991-1993*. This document has been accepted by Novib's board of directors and sets out work programmes and targets (staffing, training, women's projects as percentage of total projects, etc.) in its internal affairs, projects, education, and general secretariat (public relations, lobbying, and policy development) departments. Monitoring both internal and project activities from a gender-based perspective proved an ongoing problem, however, and much effort has been put into developing monitoring systems.

Policy formulation

As regards policy formulation, *process* is as important as outcome, and the more participatory the process, the better the result and the experience of hammering out a policy. This applies both to the development of an internal policy for an agency's own practice on gender and to the process of encouraging partner organisations in the South to devise and implement a gender policy. Partner organisations often put up considerable resistance in different ways, and it is clear that agencies face an even harder job of persuading Southern partners to take gender seriously if they have not developed a gender policy to guide their own internal practice. However, neither is it a question of an agency's *first* elaborating a gender policy without reference to Southern partners and *then* approaching partners to do the same: the two processes should go hand in hand and can enrich each other. The participatory process of formulating a gender policy, both within the organisation and in consultation with partner organisations, ensures the incorporation of perspectives on gender which reflect the cultures and societies in which agencies operate.

Many agencies have made the greatest progress in supporting policy development in women's organisations in the South. Women's organisations are often more open to dialogue and more creative and innovative in their approach. In at least one case, criticism by Southern women's organisations of a European NGDO's lack of a clear policy on women led the agency to develop its own policy.

In contrast, support for mixed organisations has turned out to be far more difficult, and they have proved more traditionalist and paternalistic in their approach to their base groups. Encouraging change in attitude and practice in Southern partners who may be resistant to taking gender seriously raises again the question of the fine line which donor agencies tread between firmness and 'donor imperialism', and the tough contradictions involved in striving for more equal relations at all levels while the North continues to hold the purse-strings. This is an issue discussed in greater detail below (see Chapter 6 in this section).

Problems and constraints

This list is a composite of the many problems and obstacles highlighted by agencies which have worked on policy formulation and implementation. Not all of these apply to all of us, but many of them will doubtless strike a chord of recognition in most of us!

At home

• The total or near-total lack of a worked-out policy, gender-specific strategy, or staff with specific responsibility for gender work.

• The view that issues of poverty, race, class, etc. must be addressed before addressing gender; a ranking of 'development issues' or goals which fails to recognise their deep inter-relationships.

• Gender work depends too much on individual people and their personal agendas and commitment to gender. A clear policy is the only answer to this.

• A shortage of qualified women staff and expertise on gender, and a lack of positive action encouraging more qualified women into jobs (see Chapter 3 in this section).

• Resistance from men, expressed in a variety of ways ranging from open hostility or ridicule, through stereotyping, to inertia or ignoring the issue.

Abroad

• Too many men/too few women employed in the field.

• Women reluctant to change, often hiding behind cultural norms as a pretext.

• Fear of feminist ideas, both in the North and in the South. Cultural resistance to gender awareness in the South, reinforced by Northern guilt about 'imposing' gender on partners or on other parts of our own institutions.

Conclusions and recommendations

These fall into two categories, organisational and programme-related, reflecting the inward-looking and outward-looking aspects of policy. These recommendations should be studied in conjunction with Chapter 3 and Chapter 5 in this section.

Organisational recommendations

• Every agency should formulate its policy in a **position paper**. The process of formulating this paper is as important as the outcome, and should be as participatory as possible, aiming to involve everyone in the organisation (including consultation with partners).

• Exchange of policy papers and other **information** on how different organisations have formulated policy should be prioritised, to provide a guide and support for others. Exchange of information on agencies' experiences of applying gender analysis to different issues (debt, trade, population, etc.) should be encouraged and facilitated.

• It is the **responsibility of management** to ensure that gender is integrated into all aspects of the agency's work. Managers must recognise that integrating gender will require taking **positive action** and allocating **adequate resources**.

• Everyone must be clear about what is meant by actively integrating gender: ideally, this should be defined in terms of **promoting women's strategic gender-determined interests**.

• The consistency or degree of fit between policy statements and the actual functioning of the organisation must be examined in all areas, including:

  ♦ recruitment (employees and consultants)
  ♦ training
  ♦ information and public relations, advertisements and images
  ♦ fundraising
  ♦ campaigns
  ♦ evaluation and reporting procedures.

• **Management and meeting styles** should become more gender-sensitive. It should be recognised that women and men have different styles in these respects. Voluntarism and the ethos of self-sacrifice should be avoided.

• The roles and responsibilities of both women and men staff as **family members** should be not only acknowledged but validated in the way the organisation operates. This involves such provisions as:

  ♦ flexibility in timetabling;
  ♦ childcare facilities for all staff;
  ♦ encouraging women and men in responsible positions to demand or expect consideration of their family commitments.

• People with **specific responsibility for gender issues** should be included on the staff of all organisations. Whether this staffing takes the form of special gender units, women's officers, or other forms may depend on the structure and size of each agency, but specialist gender units should not be isolated. Gender staff should be involved in all areas of policy, not just overseas programmes.

• However, this does not mean that gender should be relegated exclusively to the gender 'responsibles'. **All** staff, from management through to support service staff such as cleaners and drivers, should receive **training in gender issues**.

Programming recommendations

• A clear policy should be formulated, with **clear goals and clear guidelines** on the application of a gender analysis to programmes and projects. It should be accepted that implementation of such a policy will vary according to its adaptation to differing situations, countries, and cultural contexts.

• Policy for overseas programmes must be **consistent with the organisation's internal policy**. Agencies cannot demand greater gender-sensitivity from our partners than they are prepared to develop in themselves.

• Partner organisations should be thoroughly **consulted** at every stage. One way of making resistance from partners less acute is to avoid presenting them with a *fait accompli,* after maybe one initial consultation some time previously, without their being kept in touch with the process.

• **Baseline information, disaggregated according to gender,** is a prerequisite for project planning.

• Clearer guidelines are necessary on ways of incorporating considerations of gender into **evaluation and monitoring criteria**. Gender-sensitive indicators for monitoring are also necessary. Information should be shared on these issues also.

• Greater **regional coordination** to share experiences on creating and utilising guidelines is advisable.

• In formulating policy, external evaluation and the **lessons learned from different situations** (not just the successes) can help

Paper relevant to this chapter

'The role of policy in mainstreaming gender: the experience of HIVOS' by Corina Straatsma (Case Study 1)

3

Institutions

'Institutions are relations of *power*. Very few institutions are egalitarian: they allocate decision-making power in a hierarchical way and they give authority to some people over other people. They give command over resources and command over people, and determine structures of power within institutions.'

(Naila Kabeer, speaking at the workshop)

A recurrent theme in NGDO discussions on gender is the need to change the institutions in and with which we work, so as to make them more gender-aware and to promote the formation and practice of a gender-based analysis in all areas of work. This need springs in part from the perception that NGDOs cannot require partner organisations in the South to pay serious attention to gender if they show little or no evidence of doing so themselves. Structures need to be set up in our organisations to ensure that gender is incorporated into thinking and action. Some of the elements necessary to achieve this are:

- positive action to achieve a higher level of women staff in decision-making roles;
- setting targets for levels of women staff;
- in general, more gender-aware staff of both sexes;
- clear and generalised recognition throughout the organisation (starting with top management) of the importance of developing gender-awareness among staff;

- recognition of the key role of gender training and capacity-building in human-resource development.

Looking at the power structures within NGDOs to see where (or whether) gender fits in, we find tremendous differences: in some agencies gender is quite closely integrated into the formal structures, with a special gender unit or desk and/or gender expertise at other key points within the organisation; in others, gender work is on a voluntary or advisory basis; in some cases there is no real policy or structured provision for work on gender at all, and it depends on the convictions and commitment of individuals.

Moreover, although some NGDOs have made impressive progress in creating institutional spaces for gender work and in educating and training personnel at various levels, many institutional power structures, work styles, and other aspects of practice remain resolutely gender-blind and resistant to change.

Here, we look at two key points for mainstreaming gender in our institutions:

- staff development and in-house gender training for staff;
- the optimum structures for promoting gender-related issues in our institutions.

Gender training

What is gender training for?

'Gender training: the process of raising awareness of the gender dimensions, perspectives or implications of an activity, and/or planning on the basis of that awareness.'

(Georgina Ashworth, 'An ABC of institutionalising gender', (Keynote Paper 1))

There are many definitions of gender training. It is a tool, a strategy, a space for reflection, a site of debate and possibly of struggle. Training is a transformative process: it aims to increase knowledge and to develop understanding as a way to change behaviour, and to offer new skills with which to do this. One-off training exercises offer only limited rewards. The process of training should be continuous and, ideally, self-reinforcing: effecting a change in work practices through greater knowledge can lead to a further change in understanding. In the specific case of gender training, the aim is to offer some tools for analysis of the different roles and situations of women and men in development and, on the basis of new knowledge, to promote more equitable treatment of women and men in development planning and practice.

Gender training is also an instrument of institutional learning, a way of systematising experience of gender-related issues in an organisation and making it concrete, especially if it arises from practical experience. It can be a space where the experience of different parts of an agency, of different departments or regional desks, for instance, can be brought together, compared and cross-fertilised.

Gender training makes people look critically at the work culture of their institution, noticing perhaps that, although gender policy is formally approved, there is a long way to go in practice, for instance in recruitment. It highlights other areas of need for staff development, such as further training skills. In one agency, gender training had an effect that reached beyond gender issues themselves: reflecting on gender had led people in the agency to begin reflecting more critically on the agency's experience in general. In this case, gender was an entry point for the agency's starting to move away from an *ad hoc*, activist approach towards a more strategic, planned way of operating.

At this broader level, gender training can provoke discussion and analysis of theoretical and strategic issues such as what we mean by 'development' itself. The examination of unequal roles and power structures can raise issues about North/South relations, both in general and in NGDOs' relationships with their partners and overseas staff. It can highlight common resistance or avoidance strategies, some of which may come up in the course of training sessions. Gender training is essential to good development practice.

Who is gender training for?

Gender training is not simply for women or about women, but about women and men, just as gender is about women and men. Thus the involvement of both men and women is fundamental (although there is also a place for work with separate groups of women), for men need to take on responsibility for work on gender and need to know how to do it. Organisations might consider focusing specifically on men in some training, or having workshops for men. One or two EUROSTEP agencies are experimenting with male gender trainers, and the idea of building a network or male gender trainers has been suggested.

People working on gender in NGDOs have for some time been recommending that gender training must be targeted on everyone in the institution, 'from the director to the cleaners'. Managers in particular must be trained, since they are the people with the power to make structural changes in the organisation. While training is important, its aim is to lead to the creation or transformation of policies and procedures, and these are equally important. Training is not an end in itself, but a tool towards gender-fair policies and practice.

As with all aspects of gender work, initial (and possibly continuing) resistance to training is to be expected. Thus, when setting up a training, it is a good strategy to work with allies in the institution, starting where there is a way in and some support. Some agencies have found it easier to start training with the most gender-sympathetic people in the organisation; others have gone right in at the deep end, starting with the most resistant.

Some key points

The following list is by no means exhaustive. It should be read in conjunction with the final section ('Lessons learned') of Case Study 2.

• Gender is a strategic issue, and gender-based interventions in institutions need to be carefully planned. If gender training has a negative outcome because it is pitched at the wrong level — for instance if it is seen as patronising because it is pitched too low — the process of mainstreaming gender can be set back, possibly by a year or two. This raises a tactical question: who should facilitate gender training, particularly with managers — an 'insider', or a senior trainer from outside the organisation?

• Training should include both formal, structured training, for instance in methodologies such as those of the Harvard framework or Moser's model, and less formal, more experiential forms. Gender trainers in Oxfam (UK/I) find that a combination of academic training with experiential awareness-raising methods grounded in practical experiences in the South has been successful (see Case Study 2).

• Gender training is a process of continuous education, and training does not end with one session or training event. There are risks associated with superficial acquisition of knowledge. If an agency has been successful in mainstreaming gender at policy level, it may end up with staff who are able to use the correct vocabulary without translating it into much practice. Follow-up sessions need to be planned into the training programme.

• It is important to recognise that gender training is a highly specialised field. Ideally, trainers' skills should be continually upgraded. There is material already developed, but there is always a need to continue such skill-development in order to adapt to different contexts.

• Finally, there is (as ever) a need to pool and share information and experiences of gender training. Organisations which have a good history of mainstreaming gender should share their experiences in documents reporting on their experiences with mainstreaming, their successes and problems. Experiences should also be exchanged at the level of training modules and concepts. At this level it is important that there should be more input from the South. Training by women from the South can make a valuable contribution here.

Structures for promoting gender

An awareness of the significance of gender is still far from being integrated throughout our organisations. Even where gender policies exist, big gaps yawn between policy and practice. Managers are on the whole not gender-aware, and neither are all staff, whether men or women. Resistance to thinking seriously about gender-related issues persists both among Southern partner organisations and in our own Northern offices. The problems and constraints listed below are common to many European NGDOs and illustrate the magnitude of the problem.

Staffing levels and targets

Although they are in a minority, some development agencies are headed by women and have many women staff. In some agencies women staff are in the majority, but they are not in decision-making positions. But even having women in senior positions does not guarantee gender-awareness and sensitivity in working with partners. Indeed, women may attain more senior positions in male-dominated institutions at the expense of their gender-awareness. Agencies need not just more women staff but more gender-aware women in senior positions and more women (and men) experienced in gender work at all levels.

Recruitment

Technical qualifications are not always the only ones needed. Including gender-sensitivity as a criterion for recruitment and selection is important in all jobs, at all levels: in programme-related jobs because gender-sensitive staff will work towards a gender-sensitive programme overseas, and in administrative jobs because these staff work towards creating a gender-sensitive institution. However, even where agencies have equal opportunities policies in place, job descriptions and recruitment literature, except where the job is specifically gender-related, still have a tendency to be gender-neutral if not gender-blind. In some cases, work on job descriptions is being done in an equal-opportunities context; but there is often still a need for closer linkage between equal opportunities work and GAD work.

Other problems in recruitment concern candidate selection, or self-selection. Often, women candidates themselves are not self-confident. While solving this problem is a task far beyond the scope of any single employer, it is important for agencies to address ways of creating an attractive climate for women joining the organisation. There is in general still a shortage of qualified women and of expertise in gender-related issues, and a lack of positive action encouraging more qualified women into jobs. Women may be deterred from applying for senior positions if they find they will be alone in them.

Institutional support for women workers

As noted in Chapter 2 of this section, welfare facilities, based on a recognition of staff's responsibilities to their household as well as to their paid work, are necessary to allow women to take and keep positions. This means childcare provision, flexible timetabling, openness to job-sharing, part-time work, and working from home. Job descriptions should allow space for people to be parents and family members as well as workers.

Work styles

In many voluntary organisations which aim to help others, work styles tend to be masculine and to be based on a concept of the worker as having no family or personal life outside the job. This concept of the worker then opens the way for acceptance of (or demands for) a style of working incompatible with family life, even where organisations have support systems in place for staff who have families. This is a difficulty for men as well as women. There is a profound contradiction in efforts to improve the quality of life of people in the South in ways that actually worsen the quality of life of the Northern NGO's own staff. Although this is a difficult issue to address when our whole work is based on redressing the balance between the favoured North and the disadvantaged South, it is nonetheless important to struggle for explicit recognition, backed up by positive action, of staff members' double role as workers and family members.

Four types of people, according to Norwegian aid researcher Ann Therese Lotherington, may be encountered when trying to introduce gender into an institutional context:

1 The innovators: people who cut across the male-female divide; people who are open to new ideas and are not afraid of questioning and challenge. This is (unfortunately) usually a very small group and often contains people who are relatively new to the organisation and therefore have little entrenched power, unless they are in very senior positions (which they usually aren't).

2 The loyal bureaucrats: those who will go along with any policy that management decides on, as long as the tools to implement it are provided, simply because it is a part of their job. They don't necessarily understand any gender policy they are presented with and are not personally convinced (or concerned). Their basic desire is for a quiet life.

3 The hesitators: will support a new policy in public, because it is necessary to be seen to go with the organisation's latest trends. Their basic motivation is furtherance of their careers, so they will be opportunist in their support of a gender policy. Careerist women may fall into this category, torn between their wider interests as women and their personal career interests.

4 The tough guys: will mount explicit opposition. However, their position is usually clear and not influenced by factors such as career advancement. They are a wall you can play ball against, but often a brick wall: offering possibilities for dialogue, but often mounting the strongest (and most dangerous) resistance, because they are often in leadership positions such as management boards. But 'tough guys' may also be women who have been scared or alienated by the women's movement.

(From 'When Aid Becomes a Barrier: About Strategies for Implementing Women-Oriented Development Policy', a speech given at a NORAD conference entitled 'Research for Better Development Aid', November 1991)

A separate gender unit or integration of gender staff into all departments?

There is debate about where to locate staff with specific responsibility for gender issues: should there be a centralised team, such as Oxfam's GADU, or should gender teams be integrated into other structures in the organisation? The experience of several NGDOs shows that it is in fact essential to have both. However, this may be impossible for smaller agencies, and in these cases the strategy chosen will vary according to the organisation and its *modus operandi*.

Some EUROSTEP agencies have several years of experience in the practice of institutionalising gender. For the experience of Oxfam (UK/I) and MS (Denmark), see Case Studies 3 and 4.

Novib (Netherlands) has a well-developed structure, with gender 'responsibles'/advisers in each of the organisation's four departments (Education, Internal Affairs, Projects, and the General Secretariat) and a Task Force on Women consisting of two representatives from each department, chosen on the basis of specific WID or personnel policy responsibilities in their departments, gender expertise, or a central position (e.g. the secretariat for the Board of Directors). Nevertheless, like all agencies, it has encountered difficulties in putting policy into practice and in achieving consistency across different departments.

NCOS, an umbrella of 60 Flemish NGDOs in Belgium, set up a women's desk three years ago, then found that, when they changed their structures to integrate gender experts into four areas (rather than maintaining a special gender unit), they lost power and visibility. They now feel that an autonomous, separate structure is preferable. There is a risk that, once gender has become well established in an organisation and gender 'responsibles' are inserted at key points into its structures, management may decide to regard its responsibility for gender as finished and close down gender units, with the risk that gender may remain as a paper policy. The need for a small unit focusing exclusively on gender persists. On the other hand, there is a danger that separate gender units will become isolated, and gender work will be 'ghettoised' if it is not supported by management commitment and policy, as some other agencies have found. Networking and other support mechanisms are necessary.

'Decentralisation' of gender work can also result in a dilution of the proactive role of gender specialists, especially if resources are not allocated to gender work within other parts of the organisation.

Novib, for instance, has found it difficult to maintain close enough relations between the gender unit in the central office and people working on gender in the regional bureaux overseas, despite regular meetings in which they try to confront their policies with the experience of the regional bureaux.

In an ideal world, there would be no more WID/GAD desks, because gender would be so closely interwoven into the fabric of our organisations that all staff would be gender-aware and management would take gender seriously as a matter of course. But — for a whole range of reasons ultimately based on contradictions in strategic gender interests — this is not yet the case. Gender units continue to have a crucial transforming role, in:

- putting different values forward;
- setting different values on people, transforming ways of looking at households, communities, institutions;
- bringing different issues to the fore;
- changing working practice.

In fact, will a gender unit ever *not* be needed?

Integration of gender into the organisation should be seen not only in terms of the placing of staff in key positions but also (and crucially) in terms of integrating the issues of gender into the organisation's thinking and practice.

Conclusions

- Gender is a specialism, a field of technical expertise, and must be recognised as such.
- Agencies need specialist resources to deal with issues of gender, and should put money into obtaining them. Moments when decisions about structuring gender into an organisation are taken are key moments requiring not just management-led (and probably cost-led) decision-making, but the involvement of gender specialists.

- Both a separate gender unit or desk and decentralised integration of gender into all the agency's structures are necessary. The two structures are not antagonistic or mutually exclusive; indeed, they can reinforce each other. However, the exact form which the gender structures take will depend on a variety of criteria and factors specific to each agency: its history, size, activities, resource prioritisation, and constituency.

- The gender team should be seen as a resource, whose job is to promote gender, to develop an analysis, and sensitise people throughout the organisation to gender, to coordinate and network on gender issues, to act as a consultant and a catalyst. Gender experts initiate new ideas, and stimulate dialogue and debate on gender. Their role is proactive and should not be limited simply to invigilating and commenting on current practice.

- The responsibility for implementing gender policies and making the resources available to change practice lies with management. Managers' role involves integrating gender into the organisation at all levels and in all fields. Management must be accountable for the integration of gender.

- Management must therefore be thoroughly trained in gender issues.

- Monitoring criteria are necessary at staff and management level to check how gender is being integrated into the structure of the organisation.

- Finally, formal and informal networking is a valuable way of strengthening agencies' gender-fair practices and supporting people working on gender in different institutional contexts (see Chapter 7 in this section).

Papers relevant to this chapter

'Staff development and gender training in Oxfam (UK/I)' by Bridget Walker (Case Study 2)

'GADU, a specialist gender unit in Oxfam (UK/I)' by Eugenia Piza-López (Case Study 3)

'Structures to promote gender within MS' by Gitte Berg (Case Study 4)

4

Information

Language ... data ... research ... consultation ... diagnosis.
Information underpins all our other activities as NGDOs. Nothing
can be well done — from designing a project to devising a policy to
evaluating progress — without the right information. 'Information'
includes baseline data about women's situation in societies and
communities, the results of fact-finding missions, consultations with
partners and target groups, quantitative and qualitative data
provided for monitoring and evaluation purposes. At all stages in the
project cycle, we need information.

It is also important to have information about people employed in
the NGDO itself — in terms not only of gender but also of class,
ethnicity, age, etc. This is crucial information enabling monitoring of
institutional change.

Yet checklists of constraints encountered in GAD work nearly
always contain the item 'lack of/poor information' — which nearly
always means lack of *gender-specific* information. Why do we have so
little or such poor information? Here are some possible reasons:

- lack of a centralised information or documentation bank in the
  agency;
- pressures on staff time/workload, so that verbally-transmitted
  information (meetings, consultations, training sessions, etc.) is not
  properly documented;
- insufficient communication between desks/departments: project
  staff may not receive or request information not narrowly related
  to their projects;
- information-hoarding within and between organisations;
- partners confused or not clearly enough briefed about the kind of
  information they should be putting in written reports;

- ignorance, gender-blindness, or even vested interests on the part of partners;
- insufficient investment of agency resources in the right kind of research;
- lack of consistency in data-gathering: because gender-specific data are not an institutional requisite, their collection becomes a matter of the researcher's individual choice.

How do agencies obtain their knowledge of gender relations in the areas in which they and their partners work? What methodologies do they use to gauge the situation so that interventions have a chance of changing gender relations as they really are? What are the mechanisms for listening to women (and to men)? Do they work? Are they gender-biased in themselves? These questions should lead us to be constantly aware of the need for ongoing consultation with women and the need to take a critical approach to it. Just 'listening to women' — a difficult and slow task in itself (see Thematic Paper 1, 'Consulting and involving local women in project design') — is not enough. Agencies need to analyse the situation of women in the countries where they cooperate, to find out about their differences, divisions, and the points of concurrence and conflict on their interest agendas, *before* the information received from them can be confidently assessed, and then, in assessing and interpreting, there are our own cultural, political, and gender biases to take into account. Information is never gender-neutral: there is an in-built bias at both the point of transmission and the point of reception.

The importance of gender-specific data

At all stages of the development process (but most particularly at the project design and planning stages) baseline data, disaggregated by gender, are a prerequisite. Without such disaggregation, data will be distorted towards men in projects and communities, by ignoring women or treating both sexes as though they were men. This wrong information can lead to false assessments and judgements about projects and the contexts in which they operate. If details of women's and men's capacities, interests, relationships, and access to and control over resources are not available to a donor agency, there is a risk that the existing gap between development opportunities for women and men may be widened even further by the agency's support.

Donor agencies thus have a responsibility and a right to request gender-specific information related to projects from partner organisations, and a duty to provide their own. There are sometimes problems, however, with obtaining it, because of either unconscious gender-blindness or conscious resistance. NGDOs have a responsibility here to promote gender-awareness in their partners. But if gender-specific data are not forthcoming or are of poor quality, and cultural constraints are mentioned as barriers to women's participation, we should be alerted to the need to question the partner's gender-awareness.

Of course, this is not to pretend that Northern agencies' own track record on insisting on gender-specific information (and getting it) is spotless. All too easily development planners, in NGOs as well as government agencies, overlook or deliberately sidestep gender-specific implications because it saves trouble, because it causes them less self-doubt, because explicitly including women may make the project appear less 'fundable' to a gender-blind or gender-hostile paymaster, because things are easier to count and cost than people, or because so much of women's work is economically invisible.

A note on language

'Language (in the form of jargon) is often used to stake out impenetrable territory, to keep out social obligations to act or interact with others, and to avoid responsibilities to take ethical decisions. For those of us with English as our first language it is extremely important to realise that expressions, including 'gender' itself, are not in current use in other languages or do not translate with ease; therefore it is important to work out translations for concepts ... to make sure we are all conveying the same facts and ideas.'

(Georgina Ashworth, 'An ABC of institutionalising gender', Keynote Paper 1)

The importance of expertise in gender matters

In earlier sections we have mentioned the need for expertise on gender matters in development agencies. Even when gender experts are integrated into an agency's staff, there may still be a need for contracted expertise to carry out particular pieces of research. Funding good information and research is a point at which resistance may be encountered from managers who are prepared to allocate resources to technical studies (e.g. water, forestry, environmental-impact studies) but not to gender-impact studies or other gender research, on the grounds that gender is not a technical issue and therefore requires no specific expertise. Hand in hand with the task of getting gender recognised as a professional specialism for which staff must be qualified, then, goes the task of asserting the academic and technical status of gender-specific research and information. Managers must be made to realise that information about gender does not come cheap, but that not acquiring it may turn out a great deal more expensive in terms of projects which fail or are dysfunctional because the information on which they are based is faulty inthat it lacks the gender-based perspective.

A useful strategy (closely related to the following point) might be for agency networks such as EUROSTEP to share information about gender researchers and experts.

Sharing information

There is a great need to exchange information on gender issues among NGDOs, especially given the different stages which agencies have reached on the road to mainstreaming gender. Areas where exchanging ideas and information would be of value include:

- experiences in changing institutional structures;
- training experiences and models that have proved useful (or useless), both in-house (especially at top level, with senior managers) and overseas with partners;
- experiences and ideas on developing relations of partnership;
- strategies for mainstreaming gender, developing and implementing policy;
- ideas on how to 'sell' gender to an organisation in the first place;
- evaluation and monitoring experiences — not only experiences of doing evaluation and monitoring, but information gleaned from these processes about what works, what doesn't, how best to go about project planning and practice;
- working with women's organisations and feminist organisations in the South.

This list merely summarises some areas identified at the 'Enhancing our Experience' workshop and is clearly not exhaustive. NGDOs and government development-funding institutions possess between them a wealth of information on the impact of their projects and the positive and negative lessons learned from them; and some of this is viewed from a gender-based perspective. However, there is no easy access to the learning of other NGDOs and government agencies. Too much information in agencies is marked 'Confidential'. If agencies are really to move forward in this difficult and challenging area of development and working with women, they need to share lessons already learned. Things that have failed in one agency are being tried in another, for lack of information exchange. Is there really time to reinvent the wheel?

One reason often advanced for the failure to share information between NGDOs (and sometimes even between desks in the same NGDO!) is that dealing with information is time-consuming. It takes time to produce information, copy it, mail it out; there is a risk of duplicating the same information which could be found somewhere else; people complain that their desks are already too swamped with paper to be able to cope with any more. Yet there is a variety of ways in which information can be shared simply and efficiently. There is clearly also a problem of trust between agencies to be resolved. It is quite probable that gender could be an entry point here to a more general openness in information-sharing.

There is a close and obvious relationship between networking and information exchange: EUROSTEP, as an established NGDO network, has channels for spreading information that can be used more systematically. For example, the EUROSTEP newsletter could carry regular information on gender issues (case studies, agency experiences, notice of new publications or research). Greater support for a more formal exchange of case studies and strategies between agencies is to be recommended. Existing mailing lists could be used for disseminating material that already exists in terms of case studies, evaluations, etc.

Finally, there is still an urgent need for a systematic study of the strategies used by different NGDOs in taking forward issues of gender-fair development, bearing in mind their individual characteristics: size, political orientation, objectives, strategies, and methodologies. We need to share openly in-depth information about strategies that have been tried and honest assessments of their success or failure and the lessons they have taught. The EUROSTEP and this report will, we hope, be a first step in this process.

5

Programmes and projects

' ... If we agree that development's ultimate goal is not economic growth but human well-being, then a certain approach to analysing interventions becomes not just possible, but imperative.'

(Naila Kabeer, speaking at the workshop)

Project planning and implementation from a gender-based perspective can have only one ultimate goal: projects or programmes must contribute to changing the balance of the sexual division of power and resources so as to make it more equitable. This goal applies to the various stages of the 'project cycle'. Here we look at some problems of incorporating a gender-based perspective into project design, monitoring, and evaluation. A key issue, especially at the project design stage, is that of when to support *mixed projects* and when to support *women-only projects*, and what factors influence this choice.

Which partners?

Increasingly, the choice of partners is influenced by the extent to which the partner organisation is committed to changing the existing balance of power between women and men in favour of women. Agencies that are actively encouraging partner organisations to develop a gender-fair policy have found that women's organisations have been the most open to dialogue on this issue. Southern women's organisations can also play an important role in raising awareness in mixed organisations, by providing them with training and consultancy. Thus support for women's organisations and networks is essential. However, it is not sufficient. Although it is undeniable — and unsurprising — that women's organisations are taking the lead in raising gender issues not only in their own countries but with Northern donor NGDOs (criticisms from Latin American women's organisations have impelled at least one European NGDO to review its internal gender policy and practice), men too are gradually coming to realise that it is in their own interests to take gender issues seriously — even if their initial motivation is to secure funding by playing by the donor's rules.

Women's projects and organisations

The category 'women' is not always homogeneous, and the term 'autonomous women's organisations' has a range of connotations because women's organisations are themselves very varied. Some may be feminist-oriented, others not. They can be women's networks, information resources, or lobbying organisations based in capital cities and staffed by university-educated feminists, or credit cooperatives working on income-generation. Women involved may or may not be engaged in an activity that challenges gender-based power relations or the sexual division of labour. Because of the wide diversity of women's organisations in the South, it is essential for NGDOs to be clear and to have consistent criteria for whom they work with and why. Moreover, they need to be clear about the strategic importance of working with Southern organisations which have a strong gender-based perspective.

Urban-based women's organisations working on issues like legal rights, violence against women, etc. are often stereotyped as feminist (with the use of 'feminist' implying a criticism) and elitist, and may not be thought of as natural allies either by grassroots groups or by funding agencies. In some situations they are not allies, but by no means always. Women in these groups are trying to work more closely with grassroots women and to link micro-level experiences to macro-level policy issues. Some groups working on women's issues, which may or may not call themselves feminist, have a reductionist approach that ignores class and race. On the other hand, there is an increasingly strong feminist movement in many parts of the South — in Latin America, in the Philippines, in Kenya — which is bringing together aspects of class, ethnicity, and gender and challenging the development paradigm from many standpoints.

NGDOs must recognise this diversity in the South and choose carefully which organisations to work with, based on the perspective of their programme and their commitments to gender. NGDOs can play an active role in making links between the different types of work taking place, and thereby foster cross-fertilisation of ideas and learning.

'Mixed' projects and organisations

The majority of projects are 'mixed' projects, including both women and men, and most partner NGOs are mixed. A question which arises here is: are mixed projects men's projects by default, even if men are not the only participants? Is there a difference between a project which is mixed coincidentally, because it is targeted on a whole community or other mixed group (and which professes to be neutral on matters of gender), and one which has been purposely designed as a mixed project (and in which an intention to address existing gender relations can therefore be assumed)?

There are also important cultural differences between the types of organisation, popular movement, and NGO that have developed in different parts of the world. Cathrine Hasse's research for Ibis ('Target Group, Gender and Visibility in Ibis Projects', July 1992) analysed the perceived presence and 'visibility' of men and women in 14 Ibis-supported projects in Africa and Latin America, as revealed by project documentation written by Danish and local NGO staff. She found that although women were the major beneficiaries of projects in both continents, this was mentioned only in the material on the Latin American projects. However, it was not mentioned in every case. Men were never specifically mentioned as major beneficiaries of aid, even though one of the projects is *de facto* a men-only project. Latin American staff had a tendency to disaggregate the benefits in mixed as well as women's projects.

Hasse's research also suggested that there was a positive correlation between the number of women working in the aid organisation, in this case Ibis, and the importance given to women in projects. This was especially noticeable where more women, Danish and local, were involved in project planning, implementation, and evaluation.

Project design

The basic aims of incorporating the gender dimension into project design are:

- to overcome the psychological conditioning which governs prevailing gender relations and militates against changing them;
- to encourage greater unity and solidarity among women and between women and men;
- to move towards a position of greater gender equality;
- to transform development practice into a process which involves both the public and the private sphere of action.

How can this be achieved in *all* project design? A self-evident prerequisite is a gender-specific analysis of the project and the context in which it will be operational. For this we need two prime ingredients: first, gender-awareness in the people who will be involved in the project design — that is, in both the donor NGDO, the Southern partner NGO, and the target group (this can be achieved or facilitated through gender training); and second, a participatory, beneficiary-centred project-design process (information gathering, consultation, negotiation) that will give an equal voice to both women and men at all levels, but particularly in the target group (this can be achieved by developing a gender-specific research methodology).

Consulting and involving local women in project design

Thematic Paper 1 is relevant to a consideration of this task, which is a vital but difficult one, not only because of men's resistance or ignorance (in the donor NGDO, in the partner NGO, and in the target group/community), but because of constraints on women themselves: their own lack of experience and self-confidence (real or imagined) and the obstacles presented by the sheer size of their workload. These things make consultation with them and involving them actively in project design both slow and expensive. Special spaces or mechanisms for listening to women without male intervention may need to be found or created (this can be a project in itself!); negotiations and 'quiet diplomacy' may have to be carried out with men in target groups; gender training will probably be necessary for both men and women at various points in the process.

Then there is the question of which women are consulted. The process of consultation involves a degree of self-selection of interlocutors. Some women are more visible than others, and more accessible to Northern NGO researchers or interviewers. We have mentioned the class differences between women — and there may also be racial differences between women in local NGDOs and women in (for instance) indigenous communities. Whom do the women we consult represent? What are their interests in promoting the improvement of women's condition? And how do we hear the voices of the women who don't come to the meetings?

A partial answer to these problems can be provided by having more women in the field, both at the level of the donor NGDO (women field officers, women to monitor, evaluate, visit projects) and at the level of the partner (local consultants who are women and/or gender-sensitive).

Integrating gender into project design: mixed or women-only projects?

A particularly thorny question arising at the project-design stage is that of the choice between mixed or women-only projects. What are the relative advantages and disadvantages of women-only versus mixed projects, if our aim is to bring about change in power relations? Much will depend on the context: the choice may be governed by the cultural setting, by the sector of activity, by class, income group, or race — as well as by an analysis of gender relations. In certain contexts a mixed project can be more successful than a women's project in making a real contribution to redistributing power and resources among women and men.

Choosing a women-only project by no means guarantees that gender relations within the context where the project takes place will be changed for the better. In societies where the sexual division of labour is rigid, women's projects that do not challenge the established gender-based determination of activities may simply reinforce the *status quo*. It is therefore necessary to incorporate a gender-specific approach into each type of project — that is, to try to ensure that the project really empowers women (women-only projects) or effects a change in gender-based power relations within its own context (mixed projects which also empower women), and in both cases it will be necessary to develop gender-awareness within the broader social environment in which the people involved live and work. Ways to begin to achieve this are:

• In the case of a *women-only* project, by offering women a space for feeling what it is like to carry out autonomous decision-making, leading to an increased sense of control over their own lives.

• In the case of a *mixed* project, by making sure, at the very least, that women's participation is essential to the success of the project; by ensuring that decision-making and implementing bodies in the project are gender-balanced; and by making sure that the fruits of the project are shared equally between men and women.

• Each kind of project also needs a separate forum for women. While this might seem self-evident in the case of mixed projects, it is also important to stress it in the case of women-only projects. Women-only projects may exist within the context of larger mixed projects/programmes, in which women may not be the only decision-makers; women in target groups may find that their local NGO interlocutor is male, for instance.

Project monitoring and evaluation

Case Study 7 and Thematic Paper 2 are relevant here. Monitoring is the process of analysing what is happening in projects while they are in progress, so that both partners in the project can learn lessons from their experience to feed back into ongoing practice. It is both a system of checking the progress of projects and a process of institutional learning. Evaluation is a similar process, carried out at the end of a project's period of funding, to ascertain whether the project's objectives were realised and to measure its results and impact.

From a gender-determined point of view, the critical question is, as at all other stages in the project cycle, where control of monitoring and evaluation processes lies: who sets agendas and measurement yardsticks, whether consultation is horizontal or vertical, who defines success and failure.

With both project monitoring and evaluation, a basic principle for finding out what is happening or has happened in a project is to *talk to people*. This may seem self-evident, but since traditional measurements, particularly at the evaluation stage, have tended to be quantitative and thus obtainable from, for instance, written reports and financial balance sheets provided by intermediary partner NGOs, it is worth restating the obvious, particularly when gender is at issue. To be able to gauge to what extent a project is responding or has responded particularly to women's strategic gender-determined interests, we need to move not only beyond quantitative measurements and indicators but perhaps also beyond efficiency-related criteria, and to look at subjective, often intangible indicators of success and failure; and this means listening to women and men in projects and partner organisations in order to get an idea of how (or whether) projects are meeting or have met expectations *from their point of view.*

In this process there will be several points of view and several sets of interests — those of the funder, the intermediary partner NGO, and the people in the project; and there will be gender-linked differences at each point. All will need to work separately and together to arrive at criteria. The process of drawing up checklists of criteria or indicators acceptable to all is in itself at least as useful as the criteria themselves, involving all parties in a detailed analysis of the project. Even if a definitive list is not agreed, the process of negotiating it will have exposed areas where gender interests, or the interests of funder and partner, partner and target group, are in contradiction. And this can point the way to future areas of work. Thus evaluation can be a *starting point* from which to go back to the design stage and look at the discrepancies between the design and the project in practice, and find out why they arose. A gender-specific evaluation can throw up important lessons to feed into future project designs — a telling reason for sharing project evaluation experiences among NGDOs.

The tasks for donor NGOs arise at both ends of the process. At the level of producing a participatory project evaluation, or self-evaluation, or of encouraging self-monitoring and dialogue around projects, we have a facilitating role in actively seeking out women and finding out their views, in helping to make space and giving time for them to talk to each other, and in encouraging partners to do likewise.

Several agencies are now doing this kind of work, working with partners and local consultants to draw up periodical reviews of policy and practice in documents or meetings. MS has developed useful tools such as policy papers and reviews every three years, elaborated with local researchers, partners, and MS overseas development workers. Novib's experience of setting up monitoring structures is described in detail in Case Study 7. Novib warns, however, that organisational monitoring is also necessary to ensure that agreed principles are carried through in practice, especially where a monitoring system is dispersed among several desks or departments. For instance, they have found it impossible to monitor progress towards the agreed target of ensuring that ten per cent of all Novib projects are women's projects, for lack of a generally accepted definition of a women's project.

Gender-sensitive monitoring and evaluation also require more gender-sensitive women and gender experts, and more local women, on evaluation and monitoring teams at both donor and partner levels. Agencies need to ensure that consultants they employ have both grassroots experience and theoretical knowledge of gender issues. Many local NGOs with whom European NGDOs work are dominated by urban, middle-class people. However, double standards are often at work: articulate, urban-based women from Southern NGOs are not appointed as consultants on the grounds that they are 'jet-setters' and therefore not close to the base; while articulate, urban, much-travelled staff from northern NGDOs seem not to see themselves in this light. Although Northern NGDOs are sometimes reluctant to use 'jet-setting' local women as consultants, they are valuable interlocutors, for even if they are not representative of poor rural women, they are familiar with their national context and culture. European NGDOs can in fact be a bridge, allowing these local middle-class women to begin to understand and work with poor rural women.

Donor NGOs have a particular responsibility, however, at the other end of the process, which is that of ensuring a gender-sensitive reading of what people in projects tell us. And this brings us full circle back to the need to integrate gender into institutional structures and thinking about development in the North.

Papers relevant to this chapter

'Consulting and involving local women in project design' by Diana Vinding (Thematic Paper 1)

'Integrating gender issues into evaluation' by Tina Wallace (Thematic Paper 2)

'Monitoring criteria: the experience of Novib' by Ellen Sprenger (Case Study 7)

6

Partnership

'It is important to be realistic about the politics of gender. There is a mutually beneficial relationship between people working in the North and organisations in the South. Women's organisations who are partners have challenged their donor agencies and encouraged them to develop a gender policy.'

(Workshop participant)

This chapter looks briefly at partnership and the kinds of relationship between NGDOs and their partner organisations, project target groups, and women's organisations in the South. Diagrammatically, the relations of dialogue on gender might look something like this:

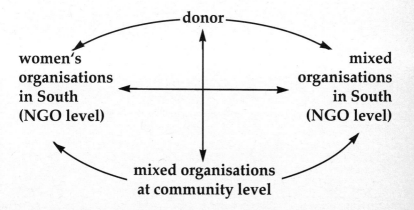

Northern NGDOs engage in dialogue directly with Southern NGOs, partners, and others, and through them with people's organisations at the grassroots, but we also talk directly to the people's organisations. At the same time, these grassroots groups may be exerting pressure upwards on their national NGOs, wanting representation in women's or mixed organisations. And the women's and mixed NGO-level organisations also talk to each other, for instance when women from a women's organisation do training with staff from a mixed NGO, or where inter-NGO forums have been set up. There are thus multiple channels, flowing in different directions, by which dialogue about gender can be conducted.

Agencies have found differences in working on gender issues in different parts of the world. Differences spring largely from different histories and cultures, and from the development of NGO movements in different regions or countries. This also includes important differences in the kinds of women's organisation and the way work on women or gender has developed. The experiences of Cambodia and Mexico offer a useful comparison here. In Cambodia, civil society has only recently started to organise independently from the state, so NGOs and grassroots organisations are just beginning to emerge. Mexico, on the other hand, has very many years of organised civil society and organisations which arose in some cases because of a need to respond to the state. Within this overall picture there are organisations at NGO level, at the grassroots, and a feminist movement.

Both these countries offer opportunities to do gender-linked work — and also limitations on it. The critical questions for Northern NGDOs are: which organisations are advancing strategic gender-determined interests in a given context, and at what level should NGDOs work? What would be the overall impact of different types of intervention? How do NGOs scale up their work, giving micro-level work an impact at national level: should Northern NGDOs support research or lobbying activities, for example? How do agencies relate NGO priorities in programme terms to gender priorities? How is gender work to be resourced? The answers to these questions will obviously vary widely, depending on the context.

Justification for dialogue

To varying degrees, agencies have developed strategies for promoting a gender-specific analysis and adoption of gender-fair policies in partner organisations in the South. Novib's experience (see

Case Study 5) of providing long-term institutional support for partner organisations in their gender work and facilitating discussion between women's and mixed partner NGOs has been particularly valuable. However, Novib gender staff are clear that this would not have been possible, and local organisations could not have been persuaded to develop policies on gender, if Novib had not won credibility among partners and defused arguments about the imposition of Northern feminism by developing its own internal gender policy and its project support for women's organisations and women's projects, and particularly by working with local experts on gender-fair development. The importance of this credibility cannot be stressed too highly: NGDOs must be prepared to demand from themselves what they demand of their project partners.

Even with credibility established, spaces for dialogue *created by donors* are still open to question. How do agencies establish a dialogue with women's organisations? Who defines the agenda and the pace and direction of dialogue? The most appropriate role for Northern agencies in this respect is to support institution-building and strengthening among Southern women's organisations;. but it may be difficult, as Oxfam's GADU has found, to obtain funding support for women's institution-building in comparison with other kinds of women's project. In some field offices, this is a reluctance to provide support for institution-building for feminist-oriented organisations.

Dealing with resistance to gender

'All cultures are constantly adapting to change, so there is no reasonable argument for their inability to adapt to the explicit implications of gender, or to the eradication of features which are discriminatory or destructive towards the female sex.'

(Georgina Ashworth, 'An ABC of institutionalising gender', Keynote Paper 1)

Among the strategies used to resist attempts to transform gender relations in development, Naila Kabeer ('Gender, development and training: raising awareness in development planning' (Bangalore, 1990, see GADU Newspack 14) identifies the following:

a. appeals to culture and tradition, as though culture and tradition were somehow frozen for all time rather than in a constant process of change;

b. accusations about Western cultural imperialism, as though Third World women were somehow incapable of making an autonomous analysis of their own situations;

c. fears that any acknowledgement of power-relations within the family puts the whole institution in danger.

There is a hierarchy of priorities at work here. It seems that challenging and changing class-based or race-based inequalities is permissible, even desirable, and can be a basis for conditioning aid, but that changing gender-based inequalities (even at the request of the women at the sharp end of them) is tantamount to changing another people's culture and therefore something we have no right to do. These resistances to gender may be offered by people in donor NGDOs who claim to speak for partners, but they may also be offered by partners. What should the response of Northern NGDOs be? To what extent are they justified in trying to change gender-relations in Southern countries?

Debates about conditioning aid in general are widespread and inconclusive, and mostly founder on the issue of measuring compliance with criteria relating to (for example) democratisation or respect for human rights. Similar problems beset the question of gender-based conditionality. How should/can a donor agency deal with a partner's resistance to gender? Does it stop or reduce funding?

A more positive (if slower) way to achieve change is through promoting gender-awareness at every stage and level of a project and through continuing, structured dialogue in forums such as working groups or platforms in which both partners can be aware of the process. In fact, Northern NGDOs are not justified in making aid conditional on compliance with any gender-related norms if they have not helped to make it possible for people to become educated about gender. The Dutch NGDO HIVOS (see Case Study 1) has found that the donor NGDO must have a clear gender policy of its own and must share it openly with all partner organisations in workshops or on platforms where discussion can take place. HIVOS considers offering conditional support to be counter-productive, but stresses the importance of being firm about requiring gender-specific information from partners and in policy implementation.

'Feminists from North and South can learn from each other, but their goals are not the same.'

(Workshop participant)

Is partnership possible?

As the case studies from Novib show, working together with partner organisations, especially on policy formulation, has had a tremendous influence on Novib's work. Working with both autonomous women's organisations and mixed organisations on platforms and in working groups has influenced Novib's policy and led to changes within Novib itself as women's organisations, particularly from Latin America, have challenged the relationship between Novib and its partners. Novib has in fact evaluated the concept of partnership jointly with Southern partners.

But inevitable contradictions and dilemmas are embedded in the idea and the practice of partnership between Northern and Southern organisations, because the principal relationship is the unequal one of donor/beneficiary. To what extent can Northern NGDOs really build strategic alliances with Southern organisations, given that inequality? In the end, the greatest opportunities for equal partnership may come from relationships in which funding does not play a big part, such as South/North networking for solidarity and lobbying purposes. Agencies should try to identify women's issues that cut across the North/South divide and creatively develop relationships that are not based on funding. Here gender units like Oxfam's GADU, which have an advisory and networking function but do not fund projects, have a particular advantage and are freer to build contacts and alliances with women's organisations which are not in a project-type relationship with their agency. However, GADU's experience with its Women's Linking project (see Case Study 9a) showed that creating alliances is extremely difficult when mediated through a donor/recipient relationship. The final section of this report deals with some experiences of women's international networking.

Papers relevant to this chapter

'The role of policy in mainstreaming gender: the experience of HIVOS' by Corina Straatsma (Case Study 1)

'North-South dialogue: the experience of Novib' by Adrie Papma (Case Study 5)

'Ibis' partner organisations' by Diana Vinding (Case Study 8)

7

Networking

At many points in discussions about mainstreaming gender in development NGOs, people are frustrated by the difficulty of obtaining good gender-specific information and by the lack of sharing among agencies of the kind of experience and information that would make it easier to learn from each other's successes and mistakes. Networking (North/North, North/South, South/South) can fulfil a number of functions in this respect, such as:

- improving gender practice among agencies;
- providing models and examples for agencies newer to the issues;
- support and solidarity;
- developing a common voice for lobbying purposes.

Many constraints on mainstreaming gender are set by the political context in Europe and worldwide. The free-market approach to development, the severely negative impact of structural adjustment, and the loss of social gains due to generalised recession all play their part in preventing women from advancing in Southern countries, and they reinforce a backlash against feminist ideas and women's social and economic emancipation in both North and South. One problem which this generates for NGDOs is scarcer resources and greater competition for them; and agencies must be on the alert to safeguard the resources allocated to gender work.

Women working on gender issues in mixed NGDOs all face similar constraints, to a greater or lesser degree: lack of status for gender work, marginalisation within the institution, work-overload, difficulties of prioritisation. By networking with sister organisations in the South, they can strengthen gender-awareness and concern for gender in institutions in both regions by sharing strategies and experiences, examples of good and bad practice, etc. Networking with partners and with Southern women's organisations and networks, and supporting their networking in the South financially and otherwise, enriches the analysis of women in Northern agencies and provides valuable ammunition in the fight against gender-blindness among colleagues and managers, as well as greater credibility with partners.

At the same time, there are vital lessons to be learned from the difficulties and contradictions of South/North networking. Oxfam UK/I's Women's Linking Project (Case Study 9a) found that as well as generating much enthusiasm and making exciting new links between Southern and Northern women, the experience of face-to-face networking brought up uncomfortable issues of the North/South balance of power, the political differences between women, and Southern mistrust of Northern donor agencies.

The next two or three years are a key period for people working on gender in an international context, with the Cairo World Conference on population and the UN Year of the Family in 1994, the Beijing World Conference on women in 1995, and the Economic and Social Summit offering important opportunities for NGDO interventions on gender — and at the same time daunting vistas of work.

These are things that affect us all and on which it is important to articulate joint strategies and a joint lobbying message. We need also to find ways of joining our voice from Europe in solidarity with the voices of women in the South, being honest about our differences and searching for common ground and areas for cooperation as women. The case studies in this section are different kinds of initiative in this field.

Towards a EUROSTEP gender network

Finally, here are some conclusions and proposals from the workshop for networking on gender within EUROSTEP, as a mixed Northern network, and for networking with other gender-oriented networks, particularly in the South. As a prerequisite for carrying out these proposals, the workshop recommended that the present informal EUROSTEP gender group be formally constituted as a EUROSTEP gender group or network.

Networking to improve our practice

• As in individual agencies, it is important both to have a working group in EUROSTEP and to work to integrate gender into the work of EUROSTEP generally. Support from the EUROSTEP secretariat in Brussels is important. Official status as a sixth EUROSTEP working group should make gender more visible in the network.

• The group should be a resource base for exchanges of ideas, experiences, documentation, lists of trainers and consultants, and so on. The support of the EUROSTEP gender group should give women in each agency more confidence in pressing for changes in policy and practice in their own organisations. Examples of successful initiatives on gender in some agencies can serve as models to encourage similar changes in others.

Networking for lobbying and advocacy

• EUROSTEP needs a specific policy clause or statement on gender.

• Women in EUROSTEP are part of a network, set up by its constituent agencies as a central medium for lobbying, that already has an ongoing lobbying agenda, principally *vis à vis* the European Community institutions. The EUROSTEP gender group therefore needs to lobby on gender specifically and on the integration of gender into all lobbying issues.

• Various EUROSTEP agencies have different lobbying targets and agendas, depending on their location, priorities, etc. Inter-agency liaison and information sharing is necessary to build a joint lobbying strategy.

• A representative from the gender group should attend meetings of other EUROSTEP working groups (debt, trade, environment, Africa, etc.) to ensure that gender is taken into account in planning, lobbying proposals, etc. If specific expertise is required, the most appropriate person in the gender group should attend.

• The EUROSTEP gender group should begin work as soon as possible to prepare for the 1995 World Conference on Women in Beijing, taking account of the outcomes of Cairo 1994 and the Social and Economic Summit in Copenhagen.

• In the longer term (and concurrently with the above specific lobbying areas), EC policy should be monitored and strategies developed for lobbying EC structures to strengthen their gender content.

• The EUROSTEP gender group should clarify its relationship with WIDE and the different remits of each network, so as to coordinate rather than duplicate lobbying work.

• The EUROSTEP gender group will take forward a programme of lobbying and research work on gender, population, and development in preparation for the next Preparatory Commission for the Cairo World Conference on Population (April 1994) and for the Conference itself in September 1994. Five EUROSTEP agencies are already involved in this work.

Networking with networks

• As the various contributions on networking to this book note, there are now a number of international networks on gender issues both in the North and the South, and some, like *Entre Mujeres*, which span North and South. They all contribute to a tremendous fund of knowledge, expertise, and strength. The EUROSTEP gender group should seek to strengthen its links with Southern women's networks such as DAWN, GABRIELA, Women Living Under Muslim Laws, etc.

• To be able to lobby the EC effectively on gender, EUROSTEP needs to argue from detailed knowledge of the impact of European macro-economic policies on women, for example the effects of structural adjustment. Agencies often complain that there is very little primary research on these effects. Proactive action needs to be taken on this issue. On the other hand, good research on these topics is being done in the South. Women in Northern NGDOs need to strengthen their links with Southern women's networks to share this information and work towards the development of joint lobbies.

Papers relevant to this chapter

'Networking to improve our practice: Oxfam's South/South Linking Project' by Candida March (Case Study 9a)

'WIDE: a European network for lobbying' by Helen O'Connell (Case Study 9b)

'Networking for human rights: Novib's experience' by Mirjam van Reisen (Case Study 9c)

'Networking: the experience of the GOOD group in APRODEV' by Gerlind Melsbach (Case Study 9d)

Section II

Keynote papers

An ABC of institutionalising gender

Georgina Ashworth, CHANGE

I speak from the experience of 15 years of advocacy for gender-awareness, usually in very hostile or reluctant environments: awareness, that is, of the significance of gender-determined roles, relations, entitlements, and inequalities, discrimination and violence in every area of human interaction. From this awareness new priorities, policy, plans, and perspectives — and thus structures — should emerge. Within this work two principles have operated. The first is the making of space for other women to speak of the specific realities of gender inequalities that concern them, rather than imposing our own interpretations — but also without what can be a rather patronising cultural and intellectual relativity. The second principle has been to affirm, explore, and describe the links between local and global issues, from community relations to the politics of international relations. In the exercise of both these principles, CHANGE has given leadership within and among the non-governmental, inter-governmental, governmental, and academic spheres.

It has to be said that there is no organisation in the world that has institutionalised gender-fair dimensions, relations, and perspectives with any of the resolution, intellectual integrity, depth, or durability really necessary to its accomplishment. So anyone starting out now can take heart that they are not as far behind as they may think, while they have the privilege of learning from others' mistakes and omissions, perhaps more than from their actions. 'Gender' is not a free-floating abstraction, nor an added paragraph to try to show credibility, but a complex and wide-ranging set of issues requiring changes to the initial standpoint, to procedures, operations, and management. As each organisation has different objectives as well as structures, no single blueprint can be given, but some principles and approaches are contributed as guidelines.

What follows is given in the form of a lexicon or alphabet, so that everyone can dip into what seems relevant to their own organisation. Politics is about the struggle to control meanings; therefore this guide to meanings is to help in that struggle in the context in which it is being waged. It is not an exhaustive list.

A is for:

Awareness, as in gender-awareness: it means being conscious that nothing is gender-neutral; that ramifications arise from any words, actions, or structures, any written statements (policy, plan) or any behaviour which affects men and women differently. It implies a willingness to pursue these ramifications, rather than note them.

Analysis: gender-analysis is both the simple comparing of the numbers of males and females in a project/event/village/office/community/ structure (even an **image**), and a more complex process of examining the relations between those counted, defining who has the right to, access to, or control of which resources, and noting age, class, and ethnicity as **variables**.

Attitudes: it is sometimes said that attitudes are unimportant unless they are expressed offensively or cause visible damage; however, they are part of the ways in which people relate to each other, part of hidden codes of behaviour; of tolerating what should not be tolerated. Although the separation of the public **culture** from the domestic usually creates the myths that men (unlike women) do not exercise their private attitudes in public, nor should they be judged by them, attitudes do bring with them the androcentric beliefs and male superiority which are institutionalised in the home and by state education; thus men (often) expect to command women in the public space, and expect women to expect to be commanded. The persistence of attacks and ridicule of 'political correctness' is deliberately intended to obliterate thought about the wrongs experienced by oppressed groups, and implies that oppression should continue to be tolerated.

Acceptability, or acceptors, of 'new' concepts, processes, and practices that result from adopting 'gender': it can also mean consumption and consumers, which gives an analogy with the marketing of a new product, which may be a useful approach. Acceptability depends on many psychological **associations** and subjective factors, as well as relations determined by structure.

Accountability: a democratic principle meaning that you are **responsible** or answerable to some one, or some people, for your actions; it has in the past referred to accountability to the pay-master, rather than to the electorate or **participants** in a project.

Association: used here not so much of a group of people related through common interest to some common action, as of *mental* association or links between different facts and phenomena, especially between the private and public, which are usually formally disassociated, though they are very visibly associated in women's and (less visibly) men's lives. However, **disassociation** is also important, because it is the way that many people, especially but not solely men, determine what is irrelevant to their work, in which they often include gender or 'women's issues'.

Affirmative (or positive) action: a commitment to create states of equality and create the space for reflecting and acting on the gender-linked dimension of an organisation's activities, because historically there has been bias, **exclusion**, and other active measures (like higher marks to qualify for entry) against the participation and representation of women and their interests, as well as the gender-determined implications of their participation and the sector or policy concerned.

B is for:

Behaviour — or behaviours, since there are many different patterns and individual acts, even within one person, depending on the context in which they are behaving. Behaviours are the outward representation of **attitudes**; they are shaped by upbringing, but, as any advertising executive knows, are not immutable. Women and men, of different classes and ethnicities, are expected to display different behaviours, with very much tighter boundaries around female behaviour and very much more latitude, forgiveness, and even impunity for aberrant male behaviours. This creates difficulties for women in the work culture, and for the institutionalising of gender.

C is for

many words, not necessarily taken in order of importance:

Culture: every institution and organisation (office, tribe, clan, class, business, political party, ministry) has its own culture, honed out of its functions, objectives, traditions, finances, sex and class composition, codes and rules — both written and unwritten. Every culture is androcentric, with sex-discrimination entrenched, and bias against the inclusion of women; this culture will affect the **acceptability** of the changes implied by the introduction of gender realities. All cultures are constantly adapting to change, so there is no reasonable argument for their inability to adapt to the explicit implications of gender, or to the eradication of features which are discriminatory or destructive towards the female sex. Cultures create gender roles and relations, although these are regulated by the state (see below).

Contract compliance: a method of imposing an obligation upon a supplier or co-participant in any enterprise to conform to established standards of fairness and affirmative action and/or to the use of a methodology, which could include gender-analysis. Although frowned upon by Western governments as 'interference in the market', it is actually, under another name, the basis of aid conditionality (and even **accountability** to the tax-payers). States all have obligations under the UN Charter to all their citizens to guarantee and promote the equal enjoyment and exercise of rights, so it is not such an alien concept or practice as many claim.

Content analysis: an examination of the substance, images, and meaning of newspaper, film, book, or project proposal, which these days should include the gender-linked implications of that analysis.

Competition, often regarded as the only desirable inspiration for initiative, and identified with desirable masculine traits related to ambition. Many men do not like competing with women, because they are afraid of losing face if they lose; unfair criteria and qualifications are imposed on women, often, to prevent such competition. However, within economic competition, **competitive advantage** is the theory of using cheap labour as the attraction for foreign investment; cheap labour is usually female and/or young (including children). Economies are structured to create competition instead of cooperation, and labour forces are being increasingly feminised.

Condescension: an attitude often used towards women which has the effect of trivialising what they say, and sometimes 'infantilising' the speaker, and therefore rendering the meaning of lesser or no importance, in turn reducing the obligation to respond with policy or action.

Caucus: an instantaneous, as well as longer-term, grouping created out of people of like minds or purpose, to carry out a combined and common function. A caucus is an extremely useful way of transforming a conference or the wording of a document, and developing strategies for the promotion of gender (see *Making Every Voice Count*, CHANGE). The membership of organisations could create a caucus to argue for and guide the institutionalising of gender.

Coalition: an association of individuals or organisations; rather like a caucus, but there are more exchanges and trade-offs involved; coalitions are useful for including and strengthening diverse interests.

Class: a variable of some significance, concerned with both relative economic power and a code of social values, and sometimes with ethnicity; however, when determined by economic power, notions of class are based on male occupations (professions, skills), and women are subsumed into a class by marriage, even though their code of values and ethnicity may be different.

D is for:

Data: which should always be disaggregated by gender, if they are to have any real meaning and use for campaigning, policy, planning, expressing the burden of proof.

Deadlines: which should be met; not doing so undermines other people's work.

Democracy: a concept with many different interpretations, from the formal and public casting of the vote for specific parties, to participation in any communal decision-making, including that in office **cultures**, factories, and the family ('the smallest democracy in the world', according to the motto of 1994, UN Year of the Family). Because so many formal and informal methods of discrimination and exclusion exist (many still legitimately), many supposedly democratic institutions do not include women.

Denial: the tendency to block out or refuse to acknowledge or **accept social phenomena** (usually negative or destructive, or which enhance the privileges of a particular sector, class, race, or sex), inequalities, responsibilities, as well as personal behaviour, which is often damaging to self or others; a common feature preventing the incorporation of gender-awareness in corporate policy, which therefore needs to be recognised and acknowledged.

Dichotomies: it is often said that Western thought-patterns are disposed towards 'scientific' dichotomies, which are expressed through our culture and affect all our thought-patterns, whether we realise it or not: in/out; full/empty; black/white; absolute good/evil; masculinity/femininity; work/non-work; war/peace; public/ private; virgin/whore. These exclude the many shades of grey (and indeed brown), the variety and interlinkage of experiences, as well as the space for and value of alternative perspectives, views, values, ideas, experiences, skills. Often these are false dichotomies, forcing us to like or hate, accept or reject, confirm or dissent, include or exclude (and to be liked, hated, accepted, rejected, included or excluded) where gradations are more real and alliances, coalitions, consensus, synthesis (and the making of mistakes) more realistic and more effective.

Durability: rather like sustainability, but less of a cliché; it means that something lasts for a long time, regardless of the fluctuations in its internal composition and in external climate and fashion (geographic or political). Many of the liberal changes to women's status over the past two decades would not necessarily pass a test for durability.

Development: most difficult to define; use your own definition.

E is for:

Economics: whether a science or an art is still not agreed, and subject to many different theories and models, most of which are presumed to be gender-neutral or gender-free. However, all theories, practices, and policies are in fact deeply biased in terms of gender. For example, consumption is geared towards male and female domestic and public roles and behaviours, and production for consumption is therefore intrinsically gender-determined. The exclusion of unpaid work is a feature of the theories of the founding fathers of economics, who simply denied its importance (something which also reflected their pampered class status), perpetuated by the current fathers even of 'alternative' economic theory. International as well as company competition operates by building a gender-bias into the labour force and avoiding responsibilities to create equalities in pay, treatment, etc. Structural adjustment of the economy is not gender-neutral, presuming certain male roles and taking advantage of female ones, including the supposedly 'free' disposition of time (see *SEXONOMYCS*, published by CHANGE).

Empowerment: the recognition from within oneself of capabilities and capacities to exercise influence, power, and leadership in some or all social relations; and then going out and acting on that recognition.

Equality: a word usually used without enough thought. Sometimes it means 'without discrimination, equal before the law or in status', and is often used with 'opportunity of treatment'; but, as women and men are exposed to such different cultural conditioning, and women are constrained by the fact of biological reproduction as well as their assigned social-reproductive roles (house-work, child-rearing, and relative-care), such a simplistic use tends to obliterate differences, as well as to render equality something confined to public space. My preferred definition is 'the legal and social capacity of women and men to mobilise and manage domestic, community, national and international resources on an equal basis'.

Equity: fairness, the application of the principles of justice (to correct or supplement the law); therefore an important principle behind efforts to institutionalise gender.

Ethics: moral standards of belief and behaviour between people, which should substantiate the arguments for institutionalising gender on the grounds that it will bring about social justice; however, cost-effectiveness often adds the final push, since the individualism of our own culture is not conducive to a strong sense of social or community responsibility. Morality has also often been identified with sexual behaviour, rather than with broader ways in which people relate to and treat each other in all contexts. Women have been excluded from determining what are ethical or moral beliefs and behaviours, even when they concern reproductive rights or issues, which have therefore been used to control and restrain them.

Evaluation: an appraisal and assessment of a project, programme, or process, all too often not addressing the quality of participation of women as well as men, because the terms of reference do not require it, or exclude its importance. A genuine evaluation of democracy, in all its component institutions, would demonstrate a low quality of participation, based substantially on exclusions and disincentives (see *When Will Democracy Include Women?*, published by CHANGE).

Exclusion: the perpetration or result of shutting or keeping someone, or some group, out of a place, group, privilege, or process, and thereby rendering it unnecessary to include their concerns and perspectives. Exclusion is probably more pervasive than discrimination, and has been fundamental to the formation of androcentric institutions and their procedures.

Ethnicity: having a common cultural or national tradition, by birth or descent (still through the male line by definition and law); a recognised variable in gender-relations — although gender is not always recognised as a variable in ethnic relations — which leads to demographic competition, strengthened cultural constraints for women, their behaviour and their rights, as well as rape as a weapon for humiliating 'the other side'.

F is for:

Framework: an outline of actions creating an environment in which people interact, usually with a purpose or set of objectives in view. A framework is necessary for institutionalising gender, and it should include creating the space for discussion, planning, and execution between all departments, divisions, branches, units, or sectors, and creating clear responsibilities for immediate and phased follow-up.

Feminism: a human rights movement; sometimes, as in 'post-feminism', said to have achieved its goals. This is patently absurd, but the term is used to block gender-fair initiatives and protect the speaker's privilege, while also vilifying feminism and feminists.

Focal points: a rather fashionable expression for people (preferably women) who take responsibility for the introduction, management, and monitoring of gender-fair policies in a certain section, department, unit, or ministry. The powers of **terms of reference** of focal points are very important to the achievement of this process. There are 'focal points' for 'women's affairs' in some governments and/or government departments; these are often men, in the still mistaken Civil Service belief in the 'sexless desk', i.e. that the person behind the desk is not significant, as administration and management are objective; and also that there is no relationship between gender and the structure of the organisation.

G is for:

Gender discrimination: discriminatory beliefs, procedures, restraints, or acts which are based on disadvantage and impede or impair the freedom of movement, belief, of one sex or the other, absolutely or relatively.

Gender training: the process of raising awareness of the gender dimensions, perspectives, or implications of an activity, and/or planning on the basis of that awareness.

Gender-violence: any form of male violence against women and girls, often immune from social disapproval or punishment because of male privilege and control of the definition of the rules and resources. There is before the UN Assembly a Declaration on Violence Against Women, with a fairly good description, which is useful to quote to those who believe that gender-violence should be tolerated. Gender-violence has been outlawed in the new Declaration and Programme of Action for Human Rights.

Gender perspectives: by this we mean 'recognition of the multiple forms of subordination and discrimination experienced by women with respect to men. These forms are experienced differently but nevertheless discriminatorily by women of different ages, ethnicity or race, socio-economic conditions, disabilities, sexual preferences, geographical location, etc.' (*La Nuestra*, Latin American Women's Conference on Human Rights, 1993).

Gender-roles and relations are instituted and maintained by marriage and family laws, by tax and social-security regulations, even by company law, all of which (even unwittingly) incorporate and perpetuate traditional or religious interpretations of 'desirable' male and female roles and behaviours; therefore all of these require constant reform.

H is for:

Human rights, both in philosophy and standards of egalitarian social relations, backed by international law, and in daily living in all the immediate contexts in which humans interact.

Hierarchy: a firmly established order of command and values, in which the top level transmits downwards and enjoys privileges not available to the lower levels. Many cultures are steeply hierarchical and full of deference, for class or age rather than experience and actual contribution. More rarely used is the expression 'heterarchal', meaning an organisation of the latter type, in which tasks and contributions are more important.

I is for:

Image: conveys the objectives and rationale of an institution (including a society, family, office, academic theory, development education unit), or what those in command want to see interpreted as the objectives and state of their organisation. Some organisations and individuals deal only in images, either by virtue of their activities or because there is no substance to their actual work/actions/ thoughts.

Integration of women in development: the official expression of the 1980s. It has limitations partly because of the difficulty of defining 'development', but also because it ignores the realities of society's dependency on women's many different functions; its concentration on women also often neglected the context of power-relations, social and institutional barriers, and the problem of time, all of which are determined and distorted by gender.

L is for:

Language: the language we all employ in informal and formal materials is important, because it symbolises and communicates attitudes, meaning, potential behaviour, sincerity of intention, and our own understanding. There are many who deny the significance of words like 'man' and 'mankind', 'he' or 'chairman', as indicators of personal and collective (corporate) perception of authentic leadership and authority. Many who ridicule the idea of adapting language to demonstrate an active commitment to equalities and the abolition of exclusion (what is sometimes known as 'political correctness') are executing **denial** of the importance of the issues and hoping they will go away.

Language (in the form of jargon) is often used to stake out impenetrable territory, to obscure social obligations to act or interact with others, and to avoid responsibilities to take ethical decisions. For those of us with English as our first language it is extremely important to realise that some expressions, including 'gender' itself, are not in current use in other languages, or do not translate with ease; therefore it is important to work out translations for concepts, not least in order to make sure we are all conveying the same facts and ideas.

Leadership: a quality characterised by taking the initiative or the lead in any location or level, once or consistently; to some it merely means giving orders from the top, and is identified with a tradition of education and training (in UK fee-paying schools, for instance) which endows already privileged people with further entitlement to take formal leadership positions, regardless of their capabilities. However, leadership on gender issues may come from any source or level.

M is for:

Masculinity: a variable set of attitudes and behaviour authenticated by a **culture**, but usually with traits assuming **leadership**, and the rejection of its opposite, femininity, or of female 'roles'.

Man: a term used for individual men, as well as a 'generic term' which users claim includes women, but which actually reinforces men as the political actors, the authentic humans, and makes women invisible or insignificant, while assuming their consent to any 'generic' policy or political act. 'Man', 'mankind', 'man-made' should be replaced by the use of 'person', 'human being', 'humankind', etc., unless specific male responsibilities are implied. (Refer also in your own language to the generic, polite, and categorical words.)

Management: the process of administration, deployment, and monitoring of resources, human, financial and physical needs. As a process of organisation, management is the key to integrating and implementing the gender-dimension of each and every project and programme of an organisation. 'Management' is also used to refer to people at the higher administrative and policy-making levels of an institution. In order to institutionalise gender, data disaggregated by sex, gender-analysis, and statements of intent all need to be integrated explicitly (and not implicitly) into the management (and therefore all the procedures and processes) of any organisation.

N is for:

Neutrality: *nothing* is gender-neutral, be it transport or democracy, irrigation or good governance; everything has gender-specific dimensions, perspectives, and implications, even virtually all-male sectors like mining. Gender-neutrality is often asserted by those who do not want to admit that they have not identified the relevant gender-determined features, or by those who want to hide gender-bias.

O is for:

Organogram: a diagram of the organisational structure of an institution or event, best when showing lines of executive responsibility and real linkage, not merely a pyramid of boxes with titles. It is useful to know at which point to insert the discussion, readings, and policy on gender, gender training, etc. To bring about the real changes in awareness, procedures and structures that are entailed requires entry points on at least three levels to every distinct division/department: commitment from the 'top' (the formal leadership), from a person or section with responsibilities for the substance of that department, and from the grassroots workers; each has different forms of power to include or exclude the implications of gender.

Oppression: another big word which frightens many people from recognising that parts of their own lives may be oppressed, or leads to denial that, as part of the privileged groups (e.g. men, employed, white, in different circumstances), they are beneficiaries of the oppression or exploitation of others, and do not therefore take responsibility for being part of the movement to create equity. Oppression, like development, is often used in league tables, which does not help the individual being oppressed: for instance, if a woman is being battered to death in South Oxford, it does her no good at all: to know that the UK claims to have a good human rights record and is among the richer countries in the world (although, by one calculation, it has just dropped below China and India).

P is for:

Parity: equality in numbers, a principle being adopted in the Council of Europe as a target for male/female participation in any delegation or structure.

Practice: common behaviour in the execution of a task, sometimes expressed as 'praxis'.

Participation: a word often used loosely to mean merely being 'in the room' or 'in the process', but without any evaluation of whether the people referred to as participating are on the margins, at the back, able to speak, able to be heard, or given a response; true participation implies space for autonomous activity.

Patriarchy: another word to use sparingly, although it neatly sums up many attitudes and behaviours, because it can set up opposition to gender issues before you have started.

Planning, as in gender planning, is a method of preparing for a project, programme, or policy which uses gender-analysis of the present situation and for projection into the future, and which therefore aims to address and overcome (with short-term and longer-term strategies of affirmative action) the inequities and problems revealed by the analysis.

Power, a big word that frightens many of us off and makes us rather ineffective: often defined as the capability to exercise control over others by controlling the resources and sources of information. Sometimes 'power' sounds like some lofty cloud on which you belong, or do not; whereas we all have power in some areas of our lives, and it is a very relative thing.

R is for:

Responsibility: taking responsibility for their own actions is difficult for many people, especially men and younger people, because of the structure of social power, the segmentation of public from private, and of many occupations. Girls in many societies and adult women, because of their culturally-determined domestic tasks, work through a process from initiation to end product (including pregnancies), and are therefore more used to knowing the outcome of their inputs. However, socialisation of male headship/leadership does also create a tendency to 'pass the blame and take the credit', and jurisprudence and the law (at least in the Western tradition) are inclined to blame the victim, if it is female or 'nature'; this concentrates on the victim rather than the perpetrator, letting him off, as well as trapping us into playing victims to get attention. Taking responsibility for an act of sexual harassment is an example.

Restructuring: the act and process of rearranging and reorganising the management of a country's (or an institution's) economy or a set of relationships, usually associated with 'structural adjustment' and therefore considered something that takes place elsewhere; however, societies are constantly being restructured by one policy or another (and therefore by politicians and decision-makers rather than 'invisible hands'), and usually use traditional gender-determined roles to maintain stability.

Representation: a democratic principle, but one at present interpreted as though there were no gender-specific needs or rights (or wrongs), and therefore considered neutral; it is not.

Rights, often the missing word from the literature on women and/or gender and development. Its omission has been used to keep women (and, in different circumstances, classes and ethnic groups) out of many areas, and to sustain male (class and group) privilege; this acts partly as a denial of the realities of gender discrimination, and partly as a euphemism, using less assertive words (e.g. 'access'), which are less easy to evaluate.

S is for:

Substance: the essential material of a process or project; therefore, if it ignores the realities of half the population, it is incomplete and inadequate for planning or policy.

Sexism: the -ism which is rarely used, compared with 'racism', 'imperialism', 'colonialism', in UN language and in current exchange, suggesting the presence of denial and refusal to come to grips with attitudes, behaviours, language, and structures which are offensive to women and uphold male privilege.

T is for:

Terms of reference: the written guidelines to a project, programme, job, occupation, organisation. These may be appropriate or inappropriate, deliberately or unconsciously (and points between); thus, sometimes failure may be built into a project because of inappropriate terms of reference, though it will be the project and not the terms of reference which will be questioned or blamed.

The ToR for gender 'focal points', units, etc., are critical, for they determine who reports to whom, how much lateral as well as vertical interaction is encouraged/discouraged, what resources they can use, what external catalysts can be included, etc.

U is for:

Unwritten or coded rules and attitudes, which often have the deliberate or casual effect of exclusion and discrimination.

V is for:

Values, a word with an immutable and rather metaphysical (god-given rather than man-made) sound to it, but one which is often used by people approving their own views and rejecting alternative principles.

W is for:

Women: a word fast being replaced by 'gender', which is not always correct, as the specifics of women's experiences, history, economic contribution, and as political actors and organisers often need to be emphasised, as well as the inequalities which are specific to being women (or girls); 'gender' maybe used as a substitute for action, a blind with which to deny the realities (e.g. of the division of labour), of what men do, which relieves them of responsibilities for them.

Y is for:

Youth, a collective noun which needs breaking down. Young men and young women have very different experiences in different societies, which are not recognised or accommodated by the homogeneous use of this word. Girls of 12 and upwards are married and reproducing in many societies, others are enclosed in purdah, most are working as many hours as grown women (and often more than adult men, let alone their male peers), and consequently are not enjoying a youth of sport and study and self-development. The implications for policy are immense.

Z is for:

Zeal, a quality necessary, along with determination and perseverance, for advocacy on gender and development.

(**Note:** Thanks are due to Georgina Ashworth for permission to reproduce this text, which was originally published by CHANGE in an edited form.)

Gender-aware policy and planning: a social-relations perspective

Naila Kabeer, Institute of Development Studies, Sussex

Since 1984, IDS has been running a three-month course called 'Women, Men, and Development', intended for a mixed constituency of planners, researchers, and development activists. In this paper, I offer a brief outline of the analytical framework that has evolved over the life of the course.[1] Our framework takes a rather wide-ranging approach. First of all, while we recognise that the domestic domain is an important site of gender-based inequality, we do not believe that gender inequality is purely a matter of familial relationships. Rather it is an aspect of all spheres of life, including many of the institutions responsible for development policy and planning. Secondly, we see gender as an important and frequently overlooked aspect of people's experiences of inequality. However, while gender is never absent (as Ann Whitehead puts it), it is always intertwined with class and other social relations. A gender analysis must be embedded within a broader social-relations framework. And thirdly, while we recognise that accurate information about existing gender-relations is an important prerequisite for good policy and planning, we also argue for the need to change many aspects of these existing gender-relations.

There are three stages to our framework. The first is a review of policy options (Policy Review A and B); the second analyses the institutional relations of gender (Institutional Analysis A and B); and the third attempts to integrate this analysis into the planning process (Analysing Interventions A, B, C, and D).

Stage 1: Policy Review (PR) — gender and policy options

The first step in our analysis (see Figure 1) looks at some of the different ways that gender might be present — or absent — in policy interventions. It also helps to clarify some of our terminology. We use the term 'gender-blind' to refer to policies which, while often appearing neutral (they are couched in abstract, generic categories, such as *communities, labour force, the poor*, etc.) are implicitly male-biased, because they are premised on the notion of a male actor and men's needs and interests. Greater gender-awareness in formulating policy requires that rather than relying on preconceived and timeless notions about gender-determined roles, we recognise the dynamic and differentiated nature of empirical reality and constantly check our assumptions with this reality.

Greater gender-awareness may lead to three alternative approaches to policy:

- **Gender-neutral policies**: Gender-neutrality in policy relies on accurate information about the existing gender-based division of resources and responsibilities, in order to ensure that policy objectives (whether related to productivity or to welfare) are met in the most efficient way possible. Gender-neutral policies attempt to target the actors appropriate to the realisation of pre-determined goals; they leave the existing division of resources and responsibilities intact.

- **Gender-specific policies**: Advocacy on behalf of women and recognition of past neglect of women's gender-related needs has given rise to policies which favour targeting activities and resources which women are likely to control or benefit from. However, without some transformative potential built into them, such policies are also likely to leave the existing division of resources and responsibilities intact.

- **Gender-redistributive/transformative policies**: These seek to transform existing gender-relations in a more democratic direction by redistributing more evenly the division of resources, responsibilities, and power between women and men. Gender-redistribution is the most politically challenging option, because it does not simply seek to channel resources to women within the existing framework, but may require men to give up certain privileges and take on certain responsibilities in order to achieve greater equity in development outcomes.

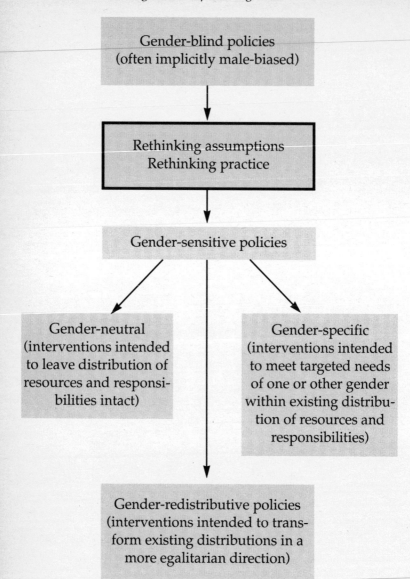

Figure 1: Policy Review (A)

These different approaches need not cancel each other out. It may be the case that in certain contexts, the adoption of gender-neutral or gender-specific policies provides women with new, socially valued resources on terms which strengthen their bargaining power, and help them to renegotiate their position within the family and community. Ultimately it is *the intentions* as well as the kinds of *social relationships* which different policies embody for women and men which determine their potential for redistributive or transformative goals.

The next step in our analysis (see Figure 2) summarises some of the official, academic, and grassroots attempts to influence the policy discourse in development. The welfare approach which characterised pre-WID development thinking has been criticised because it cast women as non-productive dependants, concerned only with family welfare. Early WID advocacy argued for equality of opportunity in development to counter the adverse effects of development on women. However, as Mayra Buvinic points out, the redistributive connotations of such arguments — and in particular its relevance for the development agencies themselves — led to its displacement within mainstream development agencies by an emphasis on women as part of a poverty-alleviation agenda. More recently, an efficiency-

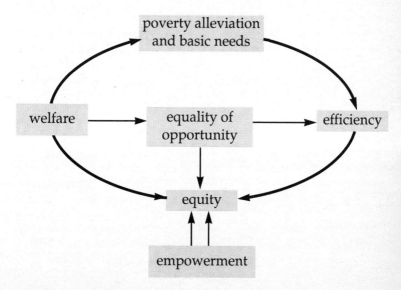

Figure 2: Policy Review (B)

oriented discourse is evident within certain donor agencies which stresses women's productive roles. It reverses the earlier argument that women needed development by arguing that development needs women: failure to take account of differences in gender-linked roles leads to the underutilisation of women as a productive resource, and carries high efficiency costs.

However, a more radical version for equity is also evident in recent texts; it argues for the need to reinstate social welfare provision as a complement, rather than an alternative, to efficiency considerations. It suggests that the problem with the old welfare approach lay not in the kinds of needs it sought to address, but in the assumptions and welfarist relationships which it embodied. A new definition of equity, put forward for instance by Diane Elson, would stress the interaction between women's contributions in building the family and making a living, and hence the interdependence of welfare and efficiency. Finally, there is a concern with women's empowerment which emerged out of grassroots activism. The DAWN group, for instance, calls for a transformation of existing social relations from the vantage point of the most oppressed sections of our societies: women who are disenfranchised by class, race, and nationality.

Stage 2: Institutional Analysis — gender and institutional relations

The approaches adopted and the interventions they give rise to will depend on the kind of analysis used to identify the problem and seek solutions. The analytical framework we are suggesting here draws attention to the way in which gender is constructed as a relationship of inequality by the rules and practices of different institutions, both separately and through their interactions. What are these institutions, and how does gender operate within them? We are concerned here with four key institutional sites within the development process: families/households; market; state; and community.[2] Most institutions tend to operate both with official ideologies concerning their goals and procedures, which disguise both implicit goals, and with informal operations which also shape institutional outcomes (see Figure 3). Very few admit to unequal and unfair relationships, yet very few are egalitarian. These official ideologies are often reproduced uncritically in social-science textbooks and popular discourse, and will be familiar to most of us. The compartmentalised

Figure 3: Institutions: the official picture

nature of the social sciences has led to the treatment of the key institutions of development as somehow separate and distinct from each other, the subject matter of different disciplines. However, the inter-disciplinary nature of both gender studies and development studies has made it increasingly clear that these different institutions, while operating according to quite distinct ideologies and procedures, also share common norms and assumptions which lead to the systematic production and reinforcement of certain social inequalities.

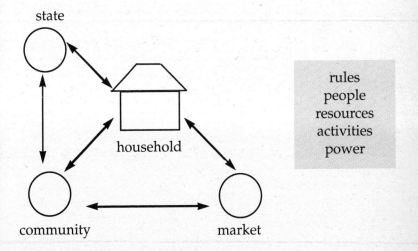

Figure 4: Institutions: the unofficial picture

To get at these norms and practices, it is necessary to move beyond the official ideologies which characterise different institutions; to 'deconstruct' them by examining the actual social relations and processes by which they are constituted. Figure 4 makes the point that most institutions are hierarchically organised — with gender as one of the central organising principles. They are also mutually constituted. State policies shape intra-household outcomes; but equally members within households can subvert or constrain state activity. Community norms and organisations can block the ability of states to improve individual circumstances. And market-based processes feed back to determine intra-household relationships. Gender, as we have pointed out, is one axis of inequality within institutions; class, race, nationality, caste, and religion all assume a different significance in different contexts as other axes of inequality. In some context, age and life cycle may also determine how individuals and groups fare. We point to five aspects of social relations within institutions as significant to the analysis of social inequality in general, and to gender inequality in particular.

At one level, institutions can be seen as a set of rules. These refer to the official norms and practices of an institution, along with the cluster of unofficial values, norms, procedures, and practices which also affect institutional recruitment, allocation, promotion, exit, and process; in other words, how things are done. Such rules can be experienced as enabling by some members or in some contexts, and constraining by others or in others. Institutions are about practice: certain things get done in certain ways within them. Institutionalised rules enable certain kinds of recurring decisions to be made with an economy of effort; but they also entrench how things get done. Institutions are about resources; all institutions are sites for the production, management, distribution, or exchange of resources which may be material (such as food, capital assets), human (labour and skills), or intangible (information, contacts, political clout). Institutions can also be seen as constituted by particular categories of people; institutions typify certain kinds of actors doing certain kinds of actions. Finally, institutional rules, resources, and practices determine how authority and power are distributed among its membership. Few institutions are egalitarian; rather the unequal distribution of rights and obligations, resources and responsibilities ensures that certain individuals or categories of individuals tend to exercise authority and decision-making power over others. Such power gives them both a stake in the *status quo* and the capacity to defend it.

A Rules (Official ideologies and goals): Regulations; codes of behaviour; principles of inclusion and exclusion

B People: Who is allowed in/who is excluded, who is the institution intended to serve?

C Resources: How are resources of authority and goods/services distributed among those associated with the institution?

D Practice: Behaviour; activities; tasks; rituals and cere-monies; procedures

E Power: Institutions define relations of power and author-ity between individuals and categories of individuals, based on institutional rules, resources, and practices

Table 1: Gender-relations within institutions

Table 1 shows a 'snap-shot' of gender-relations within institutions. A more complex analysis is necessary to explore how gender interacts with other forms of social inequality to produce very different outcomes for different groups of women and men, but — for the present purposes — we focus on gender. Drawing on the preceding analysis, the table suggests that for any institution, we need to analyse the rules, resources, practices, and hierarchies of command and control in order to uncover how gender is constituted as a relationship of inequality within it.

The point is that these various elements act simultaneously and mutually to reconstitute institutional structures. The rules and resources structure practice: who does what and how; who gets what, and who benefits. Thus, households and community norms may govern who is recruited into the household through marriage and who leaves through marriage; in some situations, they may also determine who survives as a member. Where men are seen as primary or sole breadwinners, it is likely that they will be favoured in the intra-household distribution of productive resources and claims on the household product (inheritance rights; access to land; health, food, and cash). Very often these same norms underpin state policies and explain their tendency to favour men over women in the distribution of official resources.

In the case of the official agencies of development (whether an NGO or government), the official rules of recruitment or service delivery often appear neutral, based on meritocratic principles. However, implicit bias or unofficial practices will determine who is allowed in and who is kept out. For instance, many bureaucracies made their rules at a time which gender issues were not on the development agenda. What is becoming clear now is that these rules — vertical career structures with no scope for lateral entry; uninterrupted work experience as promotion criterion; the practice of frequent transfers; emphasis on formal qualifications, often beyond what is necessary for a job — have, whatever their original intentions, ensured that these organisations are largely male-dominated. To allow more women in would require a change of rules.

To take another example, an NGO may say it is working with 'the poor' but, in reality, its rules and procedures ensure that it is a very selective group of poor people who benefit. Targeting (unspecified) heads of households, or rules that only one (unspecified) household member will be allowed access to resources, will in most situations translate into favouring male members of the low-income households. Or if an NGO is staffed primarily by men, there are likely to be limits in the extent to which it directly reaches poorer women within the community or is willing to address issues of gender power. This should not be taken literally to mean that men cannot work with women. What it does mean is that the presence of women within an organisation, particularly a controlling presence, will influence the rules and culture of that organisation in a way that is likely to make it more approachable to women from disenfranchised sections of the community.

Figure 5 draws attention to the fact that gender-linked inequalities, like other social relations, did not arise out of nowhere. They are the products of historically constituted practices and, as such, they have to be reconstituted through practice. Because naturalistic ideologies have served to conceal the social basis of gender-relations more than most forms of inequality, and because the implications of gender-based inequality are experienced within the most intimate and personalised domains of our existence, it is often difficult to appreciate that gender-relations are a social product with a history. It is important to see gender-relations not as a given, but as something dynamic, something which we are all implicated in through our practice. However, we are

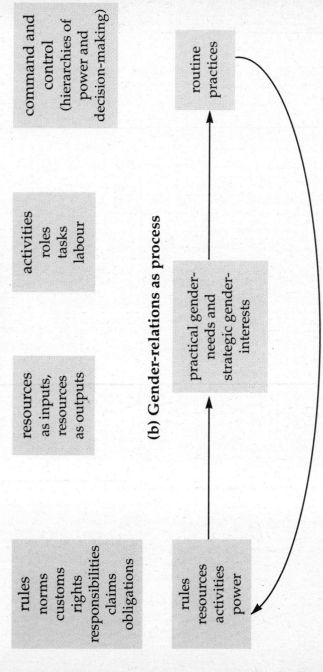

(a) Gender-relations as outcome

rules norms customs rights responsibilities claims obligations	resources as inputs, resources as outputs	activities roles tasks labour	command and control (hierarchies of power and decision-making)

(b) Gender-relations as process

rules
resources
activities
power

→ practical gender-
needs and
strategic gender-
interests

→ routine
practices

Figure 5: Gender-relations as outcome and process

implicated in different ways, and that is where the potential for transformation is likely to come. Maxine Molyneux's distinction between the practical and strategic concerns which arise out of existing gender-relations is useful here. As women and men are embedded in specific divisions of resources and responsibilities, they are likely to have certain practical needs which reflect their institutionally ascribed obligations. However, because this division is an asymmetrical one, they are likely to have very different and often conflicting strategic gender-interests in challenging or defending the existing divisions. While the practical gender-needs of women and men can be met within the domain for gender-neutral or gender-specific policies, it is the potential for contradiction and conflict arising out of their strategic gender-interests which provides the rationale for a gender-transformative approach. However, what Figure 5 also suggests is that we can change institutional rules and resources but, unless this is also accompanied by a change in practice, such change is unlikely to be sustainable.

Stage 3: Analysing Interventions (AI) — gender, institutions, and policy analysis

What does all of this say for the design of policy interventions? Reduced to its basics, all development efforts, whether micro or macro, private or public, can be seen as a technical relationship between ends and means — where we can divide means into those which feed directly into the final goals and those which are only indirect means (see Figure 6). The mobilisation of resources by which

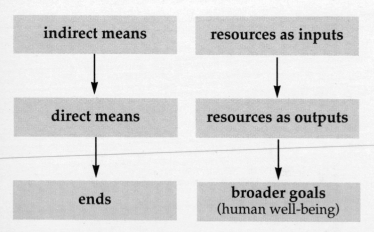

Figure 6: Analysing interventions (A)

means are translated into ends occur within specific institutional contexts. What the preceding analysis highlights is that a gender-aware policy approach must take account of the gender-relations of the relevant institutional context within which specific activities are currently undertaken, and analyse what aspects of these relations need to be challenged or reproduced, before determining the possibilities for designing more gender-sensitive policy responses.

Figure 7 places the technical relationships of production within their social and institutional context. It draws attention to the overall goals of development, the direct and indirect resources through which they are achieved, and the importance of taking account of alternative institutional sites and relationships (markets, households, communities, states) through which they are achieved. At the broadest level, the ultimate goal of all human efforts is human well-being, where we have defined well-being in terms of three inter-related dimensions: survival, security, and autonomy. The 'means' available for achieving these ends are the different kinds of resources that are mobilised through the productive effort. We have classified them as human resources (human labour, skills and effort), economic or material resources (financial and productive assets), and intangible or social resources such as networks of mutual help and solidarity, political contacts, and organisational capacity. Intangible resources may be particularly important for the poor, given their lack of material resources. Human beings thus enter our framework as both the means and the ends of development.

At the broadest level, a gender-aware approach to policy and planning requires us first to analyse the institutional mechanisms by which the different goals of development are being met, focusing on the gender-linked implications of their production and distributional practices. Such an analysis will help to clarify the extent to which institutional processes and outcomes are efficient and equitable. Secondly, where efficiency or equity goals are not met, such an analysis will help to identify the sources of the failure and to design policies and programs which either seek to correct the failure or provide alternative institutional mechanisms for achieving the desired goals. An example may help to make this stage clearer.

Suppose the analysis of poverty within a certain context reveals first of all that the poor belong to landless households and rely on various forms of self-employment for their survival. Their poverty reflects not only their lack of productive assets, but also their related lack of access to financial resources to invest in their businesses.

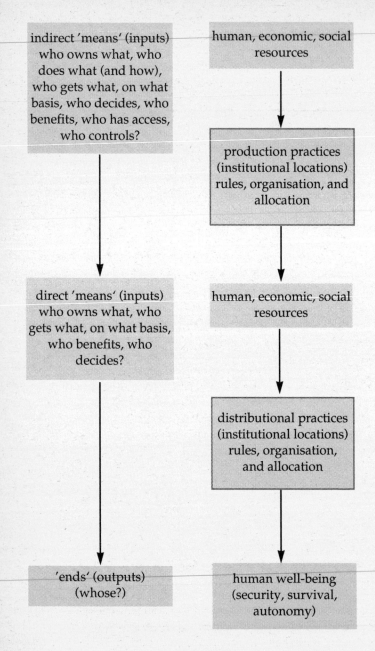

Figure 7: Analysing interventions (B)

Intra-household analysis reveals that while women within the low-income households contribute to household livelihood strategies, they are disadvantaged in the distribution of resources within the household and also face even less favourable terms of access to financial resources.

Rather than seeking to meet household basic needs directly, through (for instance) targeted feeding programmes, it is decided that a more sustainable option would be to improve the productivity of the poor (and their ability to purchase the direct means for meeting their basic needs) through the provision of credit. It is quite clear that conventional financial institutions have failed to deliver credit to the poor in general and to poor women in particular. Three alternative responses are possible. One would be to create financial intermediaries who are able to carry out the outreach work thatconventional institutions find difficult. This, for instance, was the strategy adopted by the Working Women's Forum in Madras. A second would be to provide the backing for the poor to build up their own resources: Community Development Foundation (Samakhya) in Hyderabad, for instance, seeks to build thrift and credit co-operatives for men and women from low-income households. And the third would be to create alternative financial institutions which sought to compensate for the exclusionary implications of conventional banking practices by a new set of rules and procedures which addressed the specific constraints which women in poverty face. This is the option represented by the Grameen and SEWA banks. Each of these options can be seen as an attempt to develop appropriate institutional responses to the interacting distributional failures of households and formal financial institutions.

The first stages of policy design are thus identifying problems and devising appropriate responses. However, there is a further dimension in the design of policy interventions which relates to ensuring its effectiveness. Such a dimension is relevant, regardless of the original rationale for (in this case) ensuring women's access to credit. Such access could be part of a gender-neutral analysis: women, as well as men, contribute to household income and hence women, as well as men, should be given access to credit. It could be part of a gender-specific analysis: women are more disadvantaged than men in the distribution of credit and hence special mechanisms have to be devised to ensure their access. However, if gender-relations are analysed in terms in inequality rather than just difference, it becomes clear that access does not guarantee control. It could well be the case that while credit is successfully delivered to women, intra-household power relationships mean that men appropriate these resources, leaving women with the responsibility for repaying loans. The unequal gender-determined distribution of resources has been left intact and may even have been exacerbated. Thus, even at the simplest level of successful credit delivery, a transformative component will help to ensure that the policy achieves its aims.

We talked earlier of the distinction between practical gender-based needs and strategic gender-interests. Here we see that the two become linked once the power dimension of gender-relations is taken into account. While women may have practical need for credit, deriving from survival and security considerations, policies that go beyond a concern with simple delivery mechanisms to considering ways of increasing women's ability to control resources are beginning to address their strategic gender-interests.

In the case of credit, a transformative approach would entail ensuring that women are able to retain control over how credit is used and how the proceeds from their efforts are distributed. The transformative element may be the provision of a safe place for women to keep their savings; it may be building women's sense of self-worth and self-confidence sufficiently for them to assert their own rights; it may be building their access to alternative networks as a way of increasing their bargaining power within the household. Whatever the specific elements adopted, any element which seeks to address the unequal distribution of resources, responsibilities, and power has the potential to transform practical attempts to meet women's needs into strategic attempts to build women's sense of autonomy over their own life-choices. Practical gender-needs may define what priorities are generated by the existing division of resources and responsibilities; but women's strategic gender-interests require that these priorities are met in ways that empower women rather than reinforce their dependence.

Figure 8 makes the point that the design, implementation, and evaluation of policy interventions must constantly be sensitive to the operation of intersecting power relations in shaping actual policy outcomes, and must always ask who is likely to gain from a particular option and who is likely to lose (which women and which men). The final diagram in our framework reminds us of the point made by DAWN: that it must be the needs and interestsof those who are most disenfranchised that must guide the search for a

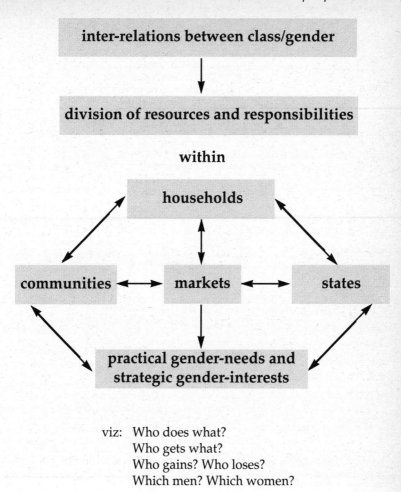

viz: Who does what?
Who gets what?
Who gains? Who loses?
Which men? Which women?

Figure 8: Analysing interventions (C)

transformative development politics. Figure 9 offers some examples of the kinds of changes that are likely to transform policies for meeting women's practical needs into ones which begin to address their strategic gender-interests. They are only examples; there are no blueprints for empowerment. But what these examples have in common is that they expand in some way the space in which women can come together to analyse, to reflect, and to act to change the conditions of their lives.

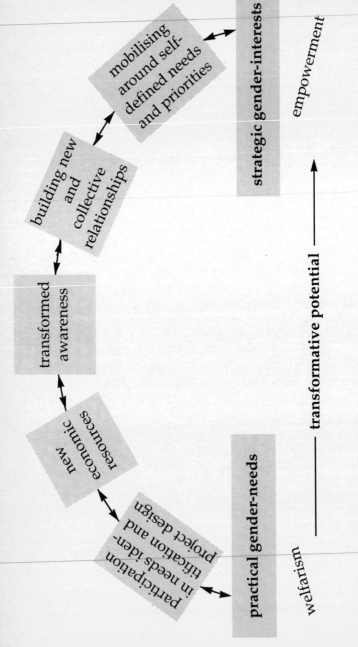

Figure 9: Analysing interventions (D) — evaluating change

Men do not appear in this final diagram, except implicitly. All the changes that we are suggesting will have gender-linked implications and involve men, but we cannot predict what the implications will be. The process of empowering women is not a symmetrical one. While redistribution may threaten men in the short term and even the medium term, we have no way of knowing what it will bring about in the longer run. Because there are risks and costs incurred in any process of change, such change must be believed in, initiated, and directed by those whose interests it is meant to serve. Empowerment cannot be given, it must be self-generated. All that a gender-transformative policy can hope to do is to provide women with the enabling resources which will allow them to take greater control of their own lives, to determine what kinds of gender-relations they would want to live within, and to devise the strategies and alliances to help them get there.

Notes

1 I have benefited considerably from my training collaborations with a variety of people. In terms of this paper, I owe a special debt to Ramya Subramaniyam for all her support, ideas, and hard work. I would also like to thank Alison Evans, Anne Marie Goetz, Shireen Huq, Deborah Kasente and Maitrayee Mukhopadyay, my most recent collaborators in gender training. I owe many of the ideas incorporated in this framework to our work together. The diagrams which accompany this paper are taken from a chapter on gender training in my forthcoming book *Reversed Realities: Gender Hierarchies in Development Thought* (Verso, 1994).

2 I am using 'community' in a slightly residual sense. After all, households, local markets, and local administrations are (strictly speaking) part of the community. However, I am using the term to cover those institutional structures (village tribunals, non-governmental organisations, the moral economy, inter-household relationships) which fall outside the other three. However, the framework is not intended as a blueprint for analysis, and some flexibility will have to be allowed for this category.

Making men an issue: gender planning for 'the other half'

Sarah White, School of Development Studies, University of East Anglia

Imagine the headlines: *Male employees strike for a higher wage. Women take to the streets to demand government subsidies on food.* How are these actions seen? In both cases, the basic motivation is very much the same. The men demand higher wages, and the women lower prices, because they need to feed their families. Their action reflects their gender-determined roles as fathers and as mothers, the responsibilities designated to men and women by culture. In both cases, mobilisation is also along class lines. Strikes or bread riots are the demands of the poor against the better off. But in media reports, the two events are seen differently. The men are workers: their action is seen as an issue of class. The women are mothers: their action is seen as due to their gender. The two kinds of movements have much in common, but they are interpreted very differently. As so often, men are seen to express a general interest, and a political one. Women are seen to represent a specific interest, which is primarily personal.

This paper argues that gender-analysis in development has tended to reinforce this bias. We may discuss whether to call our concerns WID, WAD, GID, or GAD (women in development; women and development; gender in development; gender and development), but the fact is that even if we use the term 'gender', we almost always talk about it only in relation to *women*, not men. The paper begins by showing how gender is seen as a 'women's issue' and arguing that this has had some negative outcomes for women. The second section looks at some examples of how men's gender-linked interests matter in development. The third section looks at how men's gender-interests may be obstacles to change. This final part considers how men's gender-interests may provide potential for alliances for change.

In thinking about gender-planning for men there are broadly two approaches. The first is to make men more aware about women's work, rights, exploitation, and claims for change. The second is to make male gender-identities themselves an issue in development. While the first of these is vital, it is quite generally accepted. It is therefore the second, more controversial, approach that is the main focus of this paper.

Gender as a women's issue

Historically, there are good reasons why the emphasis of gender-analysis in development has been on women. The original concern was that women had been left out of development planning. As a result, any new opportunities had been available only to men. Women had been left worse off in relative terms, or had even suffered absolute decline, with increased work-loads and decreased control of resources. The objective of WID policies was to correct this by 'counting women in'. Studies were commissioned to remedy the 'invisibility' of women. Measures should be taken to bring women into all levels of the development process: as project participants, as workers in project and programme implementation, as managers, and as development planners.

While some battles have been won, this campaign is far from over. Women and men still participate in development on unequal terms, with women gaining fewer advantages and bearing more of the disadvantages. The need is as great now as it has ever been for action to correct these biases, and to bring change in the structures which underlie them.

As time goes on, however, the terms of the debate shift. Women have come to be seen not as a single category, opposed to men, but as themselves divided in many ways: by class, age, religion, and ethnicity. This is the reason that Molyneux (1985) introduces the term 'gender-interests' rather than 'women's interests'. She wants to distinguish the interests that women, or men, have because of their gender from those which are due to their class, ethnicity, or other factors. Molyneux further divides gender-interests into 'strategic' and 'practical'. Women's strategic gender-interests lie in structural change, not only to improve their position within the existing system, but actually to change the system itself. Practical gender-interests lie in achieving incremental improvements within the existing structures. This analysis has been adapted by Moser (1989) for use as a tool in gender planning, changing the terminology, and emphasis, from *interests* into *needs*.

Molyneux mentions, but does not follow through, the fact that men have gender-interests too. In Moser's article, 'gender-needs' are exclusively *women's* needs. This is the usage that is followed in gender and development more broadly. In development planning and practice, social identities are thus differentiated as follows:

Men	Women
class	class
ethnicity	ethnicity
religion	religion
age	age
urban/rural	urban/rural
	gender

Men continue to be seen as the norm, from which women are the deviation. The fact that women's class-interests are coloured by their gender is recognised; the fact that men's class-interests are similarly coloured by gender is not. Studies of national liberation struggles point out that women often become active because they see the need to defend their lovers or children — because, that is, of their gender-interests. The way that men's participation also is shaped by cultures of masculinity and gender-determined roles as fathers, husbands or lovers, sons and brothers, is not remarked. The purpose of looking at gender is to see how what appears 'natural' is in fact culturally constructed. If gender-identities are culturally determined, this means that they are open to change. Focusing gender-analysis only on women brings out the cultural basis of female gender-identities, but leaves the impression that male gender-identities are natural. This gives them a false stability and security: masculinity is *given*, it does not need to be defended or achieved. We forget what we know full well at another level: that there is immense pressure on boys and men to 'be a man', to deny weakness and display strength. Most importantly, leaving male identities undiscussed as 'natural' misses the opportunity to assert that they too need to change.

At the project level, this 'one-eyed' view of gender can have some serious negative outcomes for women. Income-generating projects provide an obvious example. Women's subordination in the household, the argument goes, comes from their economic dependence on men. Since men are the norm, and women the deviation, the problem for women becomes (in very crude terms) that they are not men. Women therefore need to become like men, through generating income by employment or small businesses. All the change needs to come from women. Because men's gender-identities are not at issue, reproductive labour remains women's responsibility. Women are thus left to do all that they were already doing, but with the additional burden of providing income, which was seen before as a male role. It is a short step from here to women's 'double day'. Men may even come to keep more of their income for their own use, and contribute less to the support of the family, as they see their wives taking over more of the providing role. On the face of it, it often seems that the women are already doing more than their fair share. It is the men who need to face up to their responsibilities, not the women who need to take on more.

The fact that male gender-identities are culturally constructed, rather than 'natural', is clear in the anxiety that surrounds masculinity. A simple example is dress. In many societies, while women may wear men's clothes without exciting much comment, men dressing like women is a cause of embarrassment or amusement. Similarly, while women may be criticised for being 'mannish' or unfeminine, they may also be praised for 'taking it like a man'. For men to be likened to women is almost always a form of abuse: they are 'effeminate', or 'wet'; they fuss like 'old women'; they are 'tied to her apron strings'. This indicates, of course, the way that gender expresses social values. Women also may be criticised for behaving 'just like a woman'; men are rarely criticised (except by feminists!) for acting 'like a man'. Masculinity and femininity are not, then, 'about' men and women in any straightforward way. They are cultural values, not descriptions of what men or women are actually like. As a value, masculinity is available to women as well as men. It was, for example, during Margaret Thatcher's time as Prime Minister in the UK that the term 'wets' was coined for those members of the Conservative Party who did not agree with her hard line.

How men's gender-interests matter

A gender-analysis which focuses on women alone is incomplete. If gender is about relations between men and women, then the male side of the equation must also be taken into account. If women's gender-identities are to be changed, then men's must change also. This section looks at a number of examples in development in which men's gender interests are clearly part of the problem.

HIV/AIDS

It is widely recognised that for women in many cultures it is important to have children (especially sons) to gain status in families and wider society. In Bangladesh, for example, infertility (which is almost always assumed to be the woman's problem) is recognised as a legitimate reason for divorce. What has been given less attention is that 'manhood' is also often proved by having large numbers of children, or by men's demonstrating sexual potency with a number of different women. This is the case, for example, in Zambia. (If anyone has doubts about the link between gender and power, a short meditation on the term 'impotent' should quickly dispel them.).

HIV/AIDS is now a pressing development problem in almost all parts of the world. Either as sex workers or as wives, women are typically in a subordinate position to men. Their need for income or other forms of support makes it difficult for them to refuse penetration or insist that men wear condoms during intercourse. In addition, focusing HIV/AIDS campaigns on women, particularly on sex workers, may simply magnify the stigma against them and so intensify their disempowerment.

NGOs working on HIV/AIDS are now beginning to recognise that male clients must therefore be the prime target for campaigns to increase the use of condoms. More generally, it is difficult to see how the spread of HIV/AIDS will be controlled without some reworking of male gender-identities with respect to sexuality. So long as 'manhood' is 'proved' by men having multiple sexual partners, and sex itself is defined primarily as penetration, the spread of HIV/AIDS seems unlikely to be controlled. Of course there is need for work also with women, so that they are empowered to be able to say 'no'. But simultaneously work needs to be done with men, to redefine notions of 'manhood' in ways that are less hazardous to health, and founded on notions nearer to complementarity between men and women, rather than male dominance.

Domestic labour

Some African male students, taking a course in Britain this year, remarked that they felt sorry for British men: they were dominated by women, proved by the fact that they did the washing up! In many societies, little boys at quite a young age begin to distance themselves from the 'women's work' of reproductive labour. Adult men feel it is their 'right' to have the house clean and the dinner prepared and ready when they come home. They may face mockery from other men — or women — if they are seen to be 'soft' on their wives; status in the community may depend on being 'the one who wears the trousers' at home. Cultural ideals of manhood, allied with simple self-interest, thus mean that men often resist any moves to get them to share in domestic work.

Such moves on the part of women do not necessarily reflect strategic objectives. If they are still seen in terms of a husband 'helping out' his wife with 'her' housework, they do not challenge the overall construction of the gender-determined division of labour. Even when the occasion for asking men to do some domestic work is that the wife has taken a job outside the home, this does not necessarily signal a structural change in gender-relations. So long as her employment is seen in terms of her responsibilities as mother and her income is classed as 'supplementary' to his, the foundation of existing gender-norms can be preserved. Again, if domestic labour is to be more equally shared, women clearly need to be empowered so that they can resist notions that this is 'their' work. But this will be an uphill task unless simultaneously work is done with men, to deconstruct notions that 'real men' do not do housework.

Household budgeting

The gender and development literature contains many examples where women in fact contribute to the household income, but their contribution is not recognised. In the Philippines, an NGO was doing a study of household budgeting. A male member of the group was asked about his household's finances. The income was equal to only half of the expenditure. Cautiously, the NGO worker suggested that perhaps his wife also earned some income. The man was enraged: he was the man of the house, he was the sole provider. He was the only one with capital — water buffaloes and coconut palms — with which to support the family. His wife, sitting nearby, signalled the NGO worker to let it go. A few days later, the worker returned. This time the man was absent, and the wife spoke to the visitor. She had been thinking about how the family managed. Up to then, she also had believed that her husband provided most of the family income. But when they had done the accounts, she had seen it was not so.

Each morning, she said, she took on credit one kilo of flour and some sugar from the co-operative store. She made some cheap bread, *shakois*, and took it to the school gates to sell. In the evening she returned the flour and sugar to the store, and kept the income for housekeeping. Twice a week, on market days, she took two kilos of flour, and sold the *shakois* in the market-place. She had no capital, so had not thought of the income as significant. Now she realised that in fact it came to as much as her husband provided. None of the income from the coconut wine went on the housekeeping anyway: he kept that for his own gambling and cigarettes. Even when the woman saw, however, that she contributed as much income to the household as her husband did, she chose not to confront him. She knew that his idea of himself, *as a man*, was founded in his being the main provider.

Although she did not phrase it in this way, this woman took into account her husband's gender-interests and decided it was in her own gender-interests not to threaten them. Whatever we may think of her decision, this example suggests that in practice women project-participants, and many NGOs at the community level, are taking account of men's gender-interests. If we are to be responsive to 'bottom-up' initiatives, this suggests that male gender-interests should also be incorporated in gender-analysis at the planning level.

Domestic violence

A final, and controversial, example of the importance of taking male gender-interests into account is domestic violence. A woman I knew in a village in Bangladesh was beaten severely by her husband for suggesting that he should have repaired the roof of their house himself, rather than hiring a labourer to do the work while he sat idle. In daring to criticise him, she had challenged his gender-determined right to decide how to use 'his' money and time, and his authority as male head of household.

Violence is clearly a form of power, and male violence against women reflects structural relations of power between men and women in society. At the same time, however, resorting to violence is also a sign of weakness. Where power is successfully expressed, it is so all-encompassing that conflicts are completely submerged (see, for example, Lukes 1974). It is when state legitimacy fragments that movements of armed struggle arise against it and the state responds with militarisation and terror. While on the one hand male violence against women expresses the structural power in gender-relations, on the other hand it may be an expression of disempowerment. It is recognised, for example, that men who are humiliated outside the home, through class or ethnicity at work, or unemployment, often take their shame out on the women at home. There, at least, they can show who is the man.

Many NGO women's groups are mobilising to strengthen women collectively to resist domestic violence and to put pressure on the men to stop. Alongside such moves, there must be a need to work with men collectively to recover the view (present in many cultures) that domestic violence is a matter of shame, a failure of 'manhood'. If this were so, men would lose face in relation to other men, and perhaps risk severe sanctions *within male culture* if they were violent towards their families. Finally, domestic violence shows up clearly how exploitation by class or ethnicity has a gender-linked aspect for men, as much as for women. Where male violence is rooted in this wider experience of humiliation, understanding this may help NGOs to work with men to learn to use their negative energy to address this root problem, rather than displacing their frustration into violence at home.

Men's gender-interests as obstacles to change

Failing to take account of men's gender-interests results in underestimating the forces against change. The conflicts and resistance that women face in achieving structural change arise at least in part from the contradictory gender interests of men. Men's subordination of women is not just 'there': it is actively produced and reproduced *because it serves people's interests*. This is the reason for the gorgon-like quality of women's subordination: as you cut off one head, another more terrible grows in its place. There are multiple examples of what Elson and Pearson (1984) have called the 'decomposition and recomposition' of gender-relations. The original patterns of male and female identities do change, but in the new arrangement men still come out on top. Women's education is seen as positive, for example, and their low levels of education as an aspect of subordination. But Ursula Sharma (1985) reports that in India, women are gaining education and then having to stay unmarried as they become the main economic contributor to their parental household. This allows older brothers to develop their own families and careers, while the women stay at home to support their younger brothers and sisters.

Like women's, men's gender-interests may take both practical and strategic forms. In many cultures, men are seen as the main providers and protectors of the family. Their 'manhood' depends on being able to fulfil these roles, both in terms of their sense of themselves, and in the estimation of the community. Men therefore have practical gender-interests in being able to meet these expectations. As in the case of men's demands for higher wages, and women's for lower prices, women's and men's practical gender-interests may be at points complementary. Each side accepts its allotted role and manoeuvres so as to be able to fulfil it better. There is need for caution here, however. Historically, working men have tended to defend gender-linked differentials in pay and privileges, despite the fact that their wives might be employed, and the fact that better conditions for women would help the household as a whole.

Taking into account male gender-interests restores the political in the personal. It is common, for example, to find that men get better access than women to credit or other development resources which are distributed through predominantly male bureaucracies. This is typically explained as a *technical* failure to take account of women. Seeing it instead as evidence of male gender-interests might help to understand better the resilience and resistance to change of such patterns. In general, then, men's practical gender interests are found to be in contradiction to women's. The examples in the previous section provide several instances of this.

The notion of men's strategic gender-interests is more complex than that of women's. In the first place, men may have interests not simply in preserving the existing system, but in re-shaping it to increase their power. The moves spearheaded by President Zia Ul Huq in the late 1970s and 1980s towards the establishment of an Islamic state in Pakistan provide an example of this. Following the familiar pattern in which male gender-interests are veiled in 'general' terms, this was presented primarily as an issue affecting the community, not relations between men and women. It did, however, represent some very significant reworking of the existing order of things which left women structurally much worse off. Under the banner of a campaign for 'public morality', women's freedom of movement was curtailed. Under the Law of Evidence, 1984, women's evidence in court was made to count for only one half that of men's.

The Hudood Ordinance, 1979, made sex outside marriage a crime against the state. Charges of rape could be substantiated only by the evidence of four male eyewitnesses. Women who alleged rape could find themselves in the dock on a charge of adultery instead (Mamtaz and Shaheed, 1987).

This example makes clear that men, like women, may not share a vision of their strategic gender-interests, nor prioritise these above others. The shifts towards an Islamic state in Pakistan were resisted by many men, who rightly perceived them as a move of one political faction to consolidate its power. The restructuring of gender-relations to intensify male dominance was also opposed by many men, who favoured the maintenance of existing patterns, or even their liberalisation. From this point the possibility opens up that some men may actually choose strategically to fight against the dominant model of gender-relations and be ready to build alliances with feminists to bring about change.

Men's gender-interests as a basis for change

Where male gender-interests are understood as pitted against female interests, the potential for alliance between men and women on gender lines may seem small. Men benefit from overall male dominance, so why should they wish to challenge it? One part of the answer is given by Connell (1987), who points out that gender forms the basis of hierarchies not only between men and women, but also between men and men. Gay men, for example, tend to rank lowest on the scale of masculinity, as heterosexual potency is an important defining characteristic of a 'real man'. More broadly than this, we fail to understand the power dimensions of gender-relations if we see them simply in terms of giving men structural dominance over women. The dominance of men over women is also related to the dominance of some men over other men. This is present in most societies, though in some it is more obvious than in others. A very clear example is the case of the Lele, described in the 1950s by Mary Douglas. In Lele society, male 'elders' demonstrated their status by having several wives working to support them. Of course this does express power-relations between men and women, but the system as a whole is also about social ranking between men and men.

If gender establishes a hierarchy between men, this means that some men are actually disadvantaged by the existing system. In the case of the Lele, young men were opposed to older men, who took young women as wives and so restricted the younger men's access to women. (What the women felt about this is also an issue, but it is not the only issue!). The younger men clearly have different interests from the women, but their common subordination to the older men could give them a basis for alliance. This would be what Kate Young (1988:12) calls an alliance based not on 'identity of position', but on 'affinities in position'.

Distinguishing between cultural ideals of masculinity and the reality similarly opens up the possibility that men may choose to opt out of the demands that 'masculine' ideals bring. Men who come closer to the cultural ideal of femininity — of being nurturing, sensitive, emotional, and gentle — may suffer considerably in being unable to meet society's expectations of men. They may feel oppressed by the need to have a career, to be competitive and ambitious, not to talk about their emotions, to spend much time away from home while their children are growing up. Even men who can 'succeed' in the masculinity stakes may wish to have women as equal partners, and see the existing culture of gender as limiting the development of full human potential. Although building alliances with men goes against most feminist thinking on gender, it does have precedents. Men were prominent among early reformers concerned with 'the status of women' in India, for example. It is also widely recognised that, more often than not, the leaders in class struggles come from relatively privileged backgrounds. Most of the revolutionary struggles of this century have been led by people making an option for the poor against their own class interests. It is to be hoped, however, that, in the case of gender-analysis in development, 'bringing men in' would not mean surrendering the leadership to them.

Conclusion

Whether they are complementary or in contradiction, women's gender-interests clearly exist fundamentally in relation to men's. Expanding the cultural room for manoeuvre for women must be complemented by expanding the scope of possibilities for men. This is so, whether men are seen as 'the problem', obstructing women's development, or as also 'having problems' in the current gender-culture. In a strategic perspective for structural transformation, men, at least as much as women, must become the subjects of change.

Gender is a 'women's issue', but it is not *just* a women's issue. Nor is it the only women's issue, for class, ethnicity, age, and disability affect women just as they affect men in ways that are determined by their gender. Focusing on gender in relation only to women reinforces the fact that women are sidelined from 'mainstream' affairs. It also lets masculinity too easily off the hook. We need to take masculinity apart, to de-construct it, to identify its weaknesses and contradictions, not to reinforce male dominance by identifying male gender-identities as natural, impregnable, and beyond hope of change.

The argument of this paper is that we need to work with men on gender, as well as with women, if the existing relations of domination are to be transformed. This is not a softening of the line, a depoliticising of gender to call for conciliation rather than conflict. Rather, it is a call to take the battle forward behind the enemy lines, and be prepared to find there perhaps unexpected allies.

References

Connell, R. (1987), *Gender and Power*, Oxford: Polity Press.

Elson, D. and **R. Pearson** (1984), 'The subordination of women and the internationalisation of factory production', in Kate Young (ed.): *Of Marriage and the Market*, London: Routledge.

Lukes, S. (1974), *Power: A Radical View*, London: Macmillan.

Mamtaz, M. and **F. Shaheed** (1987), *Women in Pakistan: Two Steps Forward, One Step Back*, London: Zed.

Molyneux, M. (1985), 'Mobilisation without emancipation? Women's interests, the state, and revolution in Nicaragua', *Feminist Studies* 11 (2):227-54.

Moser, Caroline (1989), 'Gender planning in the Third World: meeting practical and strategic gender needs', *World Development* 17 (11):1799-825.

Sharma, U. (1985), 'Unmarried women and the household economy: a research note', *Journal of Social Studies* 20: 1-12 (Dhaka).

Young, K. (1988), 'Reflections on meeting women's needs', in Young (ed.): *Women and Economic Development: Local, Regional and National Planning Strategies*, Oxford: Berg/UNESCO.

Thematic papers

Consulting and involving local women in project design

Diana Vinding, IBIS

Ibis's experience of consulting and involving local women in project design has been limited to date. There has in fact been no consultation or involvement of women in the design stage, at the outset of the project, and project-feasibility studies have been too short to allow for a deeper analysis. However, we have tried to consult women in greater depth in the course of projects. We carry out interviews during project appraisal, do baseline studies, and facilitate self-analysis and self-evaluation by project partners themselves.

Latin America is the continent where Ibis has had the broadest experience of women's projects and involving women in various stages of project management, in a variety of urban and rural sectors: agriculture, health, income generation, garment-making, community-development projects in slums and shanty towns, training women trade-union leaders, and non-traditional work such as a factory making wooden furniture with women workers only.

In the following account, the two processes of consulting local women and involving them in project design will be analysed separately. Both processes are subject to difficulties that relate to three different sources: difficulties related to men; difficulties related to women; and difficulties related to specific factors such as religion or language.

Consulting local women

Problems

Difficulties related to men are encountered at organisational level, both within Ibis and with NGO partners. Feminism is seen as a threat to family values, especially in rural areas. Both here and at community level, men are not interested in letting women speak, and may indeed fear that consultation with women will somehow be to their disadvantage. They prefer to participate themselves, to take the lead in discussion and speak for women.

This difficulty is also found at household level, where men do not let women speak for themselves, or insist on being present during interviews with women. It is very difficult to interview women alone. On the other hand, women in many cases leave the talking to men and defer to them in discussions, for a variety of reasons. They may simply share the traditional outlook of their menfolk. They may feel insecure and unconfident through lack of education and lack of practice in speaking for themselves, or shy about talking to unfamiliar people. There are also particular difficulties for women in taking time out from work in order to engage in discussion, and they may lack their own spaces within the community or be unable to leave it for meetings elsewhere.

A further, general difficulty in project design is that most projects lack good baseline information — particularly information disaggregated by gender — about the target-group's living conditions, capacities, and potential for different kinds of work. It is crucial to have such information at the project design stage, and to get it by consultation with the target group as well as with local NGOs.

Strategies

There are several sets of strategies to overcome these difficulties. The first set is strategies of **approach**. The team involved in the project design should have a gender-aware team leader or include a gender expert. This will ensure that the aspect of gender is built into documentation such as project proposals. With partners, a useful strategy is to use human rights as an argument, backed up by reference to recent EC policy statements on the close relationship between development and human rights. Male community leaders can be approached first and informed how and why women are going to be consulted. This can reduce the threat to their interests which men in the community may feel. Then natural leaders among the women in the community (such as midwives and older women) can be approached.

The second set is strategies of **methodology**. A fundamental one is to use women researchers and investigators. Question-naires, interviews, and self-analyses can also be designed from a gender-linked perspective, so as to establish a dialogue that lets women articulate their own problems and suggest solutions springing from their own experience and knowledge. It is possible to make sure that women's voices are heard without male censorship or interference, for instance:

- by contacting women at hours when they are alone, or arranging for group meetings without men being present (this may involve prior negotiation with male community leaders, see above);
- by contacting women at or near their homes;
- by using a female interpreter wherever possible;
- by using a person from the same language group.

Ibis has found the **self-analysis approach** particularly suitable, and many NGOs now use this methodology. Ibis always uses it for consultations with women, but it could be done with men as well. However, it has to be acknowledged that it is a time-consuming process. Women have to be trained to consult and to process their findings. But the process is extremely worth-while and is empowering for the women who participate in it.

Involving local women

Problems

Difficulties related to men at the organisational level (within Ibis and partners) arise chiefly from lack of knowledge. Men often do not know enough about the specificities of women's situation to be able to assess women's needs (let alone their interests) accurately. They may also lack the necessary motivation to adopt appropriate methods to get women on to an equal footing with men, such as training and appropriate technology.

At community level, men tend to feel threatened when women are brought into the project-design process. Constraints may spring from men's fear of having to surrender their disproportionate share of the advantages of the project. They may resent the amount of resources directed to women, and may try to co-opt project resources for themselves. Often, men in the community express a lack of trust in women's physical and mental capabilities to carry out tasks, for instance to earn a salary in an agricultural cooperative. And they fear losing authority in the community.

Similar emotions come into play at the household level, where men fear losing authority as heads of households. They will argue that if women are involved actively in development projects they will no longer be able (i.e. willing) to look after the house. They may bring to bear moralistic arguments about the disruption of family life entailed in women's even partial absence from the house and commitments outside the close family circle. They may express jealousy of other men (for example,. project colleagues of the women) if their own control over the women of the household is weakened.

Difficulties related to women in the community spring from women's tendency to accept men's valuation of their work and their capabilities, often in the face of empirical evidence to the contrary. Thus the objections they may raise to getting involved in the project may be real or imagined, for example when they say they have not enough time or mobility to get away from the home. It is difficult to overcome women's acceptance of men's domination. Deference to men also exacerbates shyness or fear in women when they meet unfamiliar men, and especially foreign men from donor agencies (or sometimes partner NGOs).

Other difficulties related to women concern their unequal access to education and training, which often results in a limited vision of what they can, or may, achieve as women. Women tend to be uninterested in the design and planning aspects of a project, which they see as 'abstract learning'; they prefer to get started with the activity at once. This also means that they may lack a long-term view of the project and its potential benefits and thus be more concerned with meeting practical needs than with considering strategic needs or interests. Moreover, they have a limited understanding of the possibilities open to them, seeing 'women's projects', for instance, solely in terms of sewing, income generation through preparing and selling food, or running a beauty parlour as the only appropriate work for them.

Finally, women suffer constraints springing from religion or traditional custom which prohibit them from carrying out certain activities on the grounds of religion or taboo. Language can also play a part: often the women in a rural community speak only the indigenous language and not whichever European language is used as the main medium for dealing with local and international NGOs.

Strategies

The donor NGDO has to aim to avoid competition between men and women for project resources and control, at the same time being aware that some kind of affirmative action is required because women are *a priori* handicapped in any such competition. A checklist of strategies to ensure a more equal representation of women and men at all levels in decision-making about the project could include the following:

To minimise men's unequal control over the project

- Make sure that the project leader is gender-aware and that there is a 'gender responsible' on the project team.
- Reserve a percentage of each funding budget line from the start for women-oriented activities.
- Demand that elections be held for both a man and a woman on the project committee.
- Inform both men and women about women's situation. Often there is a tendency to inform only women about their rights, but men cannot be expected to understand women's demands if they do not know on what they are based.
- Educate both men and women to recognise the value of women's reproductive and productive work (invisible work in the home).
- Keep men informed about the women's activities, possibly inviting them to some meetings and activities of the women (while remaining aware of the need for women to have exclusive spaces).
- Incorporate women's aspects in training and education activities for men, and *vice versa*.

To maximise women's involvement

- Decentralise activities and training in order to overcome women's mobility problems: take the activities to the women, if you can't bring the women to the activities. Alternatively, arrange for special facilities (childcare, food provision, etc.) if the activities take place at a central location.

• Adapt activities and training for women who are illiterate; and/or combine literacy with practical training (functional literacy).

• Create specific women's forums where women can express themselves freely, and involve women in women-only activities.

• Use a facilitator to allow women to speak in mixed meetings.

• Make sure that women's activities are included and maintained in projects via thorough feasibility studies, monitoring, and ongoing support.

• Use female extension workers.

• Listen to women's expressed wishes, even if these reflect a focus on traditional 'women's activities' such as dressmaking, beauty care, etc. Capitalise on the motivation for these activities to introduce and promote activities with a more strategic perspective.

• At the same time, we must be aware that certain barriers are impossible or extremely difficult to overcome, such as women's physical limitations, or expecting women to work on night shifts together with men. Plan for alternative solutions.

To overcome specific barriers created by language, religion, and taboo

• Arrange for women-only activities, possibly held in homes or places where women feel safe.

• Use extensionists from the same language group or cultural background.

• Make use of traditional knowledge whenever possible, and respect 'superstitions' and taboos — but being aware, at the same time, that these may conflict with gender-fair development.

Integrating gender issues into evaluation

Tina Wallace, Oxfam (UK and Ireland)

What is evaluation? Traditionally, it is the tool we have for measuring the outcome of project. (We are talking here only about the project level, not programme level.) The kinds of question that are asked in evaluation are:

- Were the objectives achieved?
- What were the results?
- What was the impact of this project?

Most evaluation has focused on quantifiable, measurable results: how much money was made, how much did it cost, how many people were reached, how many trainings were held, and so on. But the current emphasis is on such questions as:

- Was the project relevant to the problem?
- Was it delivered efficiently (which usually means, not too expensively)?
- Was it effective in terms of impact? Were the right things done at the right time, and did they have the impact we wanted?

And, of course, we now always need to ask:

- Is the project sustainable?

Who defines?

These questions are all very valid ones, but if we are talking about evaluation which has meaning for the people who are involved in the project, and which has meaning for women, there are several critical issues to address. The most critical issue is, *who is defining these criteria?* Who says whether the project was relevant or not? Who says whether it has had an impact that was good or bad?

This is the point at which we must start to consider the different people who participate in projects. All kinds of different interests are at stake. Often the *funders* have one set of definitions of what is relevant, what is efficient, what is effective, and so on; while the *intermediary agencies*, whether they are international NGOs or local NGOs, also have their own agendas and their own ideas about what would be good for this project to achieve. Even local NGOs often have a different agenda from the participants in the project. At the next level are the *beneficiaries*, the people who are actually part of it, who will often have a different set of criteria, their own indicators to measure the achievements of the project, to judge whether it met their needs or not. And within all those groups, there will be a difference in understanding and perception, very often, between *men and women*.

Here I particularly want to focus on the beneficiaries. Evaluations need to be focused on the needs of the beneficiaries, both women and men, and use the criteria and definitions of success and failure defined by them. Women and men in projects do not share the same responsibilities, they don't play the same roles, they don't have to achieve the same things; and therefore their definitions of what makes a good project or a bad project are often very different. Projects that may be deemed entirely successful by the men because they increase productivity may have had a very negative impact on the women, because they have increased their labour or taken land out of their control.

So the heart of the matter is the question: who is setting up the indicators? Who is setting up the criteria by which we are going to evaluate the success or failure of a project? The funders cannot do this on their own, and the implementers cannot do it on their own, without knowing what the impact was on men and women — and it will very often be different at the project level.

What enables good gender-aware evaluation?

Obviously, evaluation comes at the end of a process of project management, so what makes it possible for us to do good evaluation at the end of a project is determined by a number of factors, starting back at the planning stage. Unless the project has been planned well, evaluating it will probably be a waste of time, because all you will find is that it wasn't planned well, and so it didn't work. Before we can evaluate a project from a gender-based perspective, several things are necessary:

• A well-planned project needs to have clear objectives, and it needs good indicators to judge if it has reached those objectives. These have to be negotiated with women and men. Sometimes this has to be done separately, because women and men can't work together; sometimes it can be done together. But the whole process, from the beginning, involves this kind of negotiating with women and men at project level.

• We also need good information about the roles, responsibilities, and the resources available to men and women separately. This information has to be disaggregated by gender — although some of these things can be relevant to class and race, too, depending on the context. Good, disaggregated baseline data are often lacking. But without a clear understanding of the position of men and women, it will be very difficult, first of all to decide whether the project was relevant to them, and secondly whether the project made any impact on them. This is an area where I think many NGOs are extremely weak.

• If projects are to be designed so as to be relevant and efficient, we have to understand what the problem is that people want to solve with the project. What is it that they want to achieve? Again, to understand that, we have to understand that there might be different perspectives. Communities, villages, and groups are not homogeneous; women and men may very often have different perspectives, and both have to be looked at and accommodated as far as possible.

• On-going monitoring is necessary, involving both women and men. If your evaluation is to be done from a gender-based perspective, the monitoring must have been done from that perspective as well. This is the phase where objectives and indicators can be reviewed, and changed or adapted if necessary. Often it will be found that the donors, the intermediary NGOs, or even the project beneficiaries haven't got the project quite right, if it is to do what they want it to do. Again, this process needs to involve both women and men.

• The final precondition for a gender-sensitive evaluation is that women as well as men must be able to participate in the evaluation. This is far easier said than done.

What are the barriers to women's participation?

All of these stages are actually about involving women as well as men in the project, right from the design stage through to evaluation. But the whole language of projects and the way they are implemented militate against women's being involved. So we must look at the barriers to achieving a gender-sensitive evaluation -- and, indeed, a gender-sensitive project.

It is important to remember that we can talk about women's participation and the importance of women's involvement and of hearing their views, but there are all sorts of constraints preventing them from participating fully: lack of time; heavy workloads; lack of confidence; unfamiliarity with the language and concepts of project planning; fear of outsiders; and religious and other cultural restrictions.

This is obviously a very incomplete list, and it should probably be headed 'Attitudes of NGOs': often the barriers to women's involvement is the way in which the project is being implemented. Another barrier is men's attitudes to women.

Can we overcome these barriers to women's involvement? How can women attend meetings on top of their other work? What kind of childcare or alternative labour can we provide in order for them to come? Lack of confidence among women goes right through from the beneficiaries to the funding agencies: women lack the confidence to speak, they aren't used to articulating their views, they don't have the experience to do so. The language of projects is not the everyday language of people at village level, particularly not the everyday language of women. The whole way we approach women can be a barrier.

Finding ways to overcome these barriers

If we cannot design good projects unless women are involved, and if we can evaluate them well only if women are involved, there is an enormous amount of work to be done. At the most general level, are we looking at the way we design projects? Are we looking at the way we approach people on projects, how project documents have to be filled in, what requirements we are making?

These are some more specific ways to overcome barriers to women's involvement:

- training to make our own staff aware of how to work with women;
- training women at village level, or whatever level we are working at, using a number of different trainings, from literacy to management to public speaking;
- finding times when women can actually attend;
- in some circumstances, having meetings for women only — that may be the only forum in which they feel confident of speaking (even inside our own institutions, many women staff feel far more confident about speaking when there are only, or mainly, women present);
- being more creative and imaginative about the methodologies we use, for example adapting some of the participatory rural appraisal (PRA) techniques that were developed for trying to listen better to village people during research at village level.

It is worth noting in passing that a lot of these things are not done to ensure the participation of men either, at the moment.

Methodologies for gender evaluation and planning

Let us take a brief look at some of the methodologies for gender evaluation and planning, some of the ways of making sure that women and men are adequately involved. First, the basic principle, which is quite simple: it consists of *talking* to people. This sounds obvious, but it's often not done. Second, we need to understand the roles, responsibilities, and rights of women: their position in the household and the community, the opportunities there are for them, and the constraints they face. The third consideration is the 'entry strategy': when you meet a group, see the meeting as a negotiation, see it as a dialogue where you have to work out between you what the goals of the project are. If it's a project with men and women, it has to be agreed between the men, and the women, and the implementer, and the funder. This is not a simple relationship. It has to be clear who is going to play what role. We're always very clear about what role the village people have to play; we're usually less clear about our role in the process. A kind of contract has to be set up where it is clear what the women will do, what the men will do, what we're going to do to support the women, etc. Make sure you do end up with a shared analysis of the problem, and look at ways to develop women's participation.

There are three more academically developed tools to help us with gender planning and evaluation. One was devised by Sarah Longwe, who is based in Zambia. Her criteria measure the extent to which a given project promotes:

- women's welfare;
- women's access;
- women's conscientisation;
- women's participation;
- women's control.

Another set of tools is the Maxine Molyneux/Caroline Moser model; and the third is the Harvard framework of analysis. I will not deal with these in detail, but I mention them to make the point that there are tools that have been developed by people working in this field and that we can use: we don't have to reinvent the wheel each time.

Some conclusions

1 Evaluation taking gender into account can be done well only if gender-related considerations have been integral from the planning stage onwards.

2 Gender planning, monitoring, and evaluation all require the *active involvement of women*. This is not an optional extra. It is essential to the design of good projects; and therefore the onus is on agencies at all levels to find ways to overcome the barriers to women's involvement and participation at the level of the beneficiaries, the local NGOs, and the funding agencies.

3 Evaluation must look at the success of a project from a number of perspectives: how the project was organised, who participated, what the impact was. To do this, cost-benefit analyses and quantitative indicators are insufficient. We must become more confident about using *subjective or 'soft' indicators of success and failure*. The indicator has to be generated within the project; but

we are still new to these ideas and are not very clear about what our approach to subjective indicators is. The guiding principle for developing these indicators is that beneficiaries, local NGOs, and funders may all have different criteria, and men may well have different criteria from women; so we have to work together to elicit clear objectives and indicators, or proxy indicators, from all the stakeholders in a project. Where there are conflicts, these have to be negotiated.

4 At a more concrete level, when undertaking evaluations, funders, NGOs, and consultants must write *gender-sensitive terms of reference* and recruit people who are capable of implementing those terms of reference. The teams must be able to communicate; they must include women, so as to be accessible to women; but they must also be people who understand the gender dimension. It is very important to allow enough *time to listen to women*. It is usually impossible to canvass the views and responses of women in a one-week or two-week evaluation. We must recognise that there is a cost in involving women: we have to work at a different pace and include different people in the process; and this doesn't come free.

5 More work needs to be done to *evaluate projects which have already been set up from a gender perspective* and where women as well as men have been involved throughout the project cycle. There are a few such projects in existence, but it is very difficult to find any evaluations of them. Those of us who are promoting a gender-based perspective now need to go out and evaluate these gender-sensitive projects to see whether they've worked any better. The question being asked now is: if an agency invests more time and money in a gender-sensitive project, will it end up with a better impact? We don't have the answer to this question yet, because evaluations of such projects are few and far between. The HIVOS studies are thus especially valuable as systematic attempts to look back at how NGOs are working with issues of gender.

6 More work needs to be done in different contexts on how to work with women to *involve them more in projects from the planning stage right through to evaluation*; how to tackle the barriers inhibiting their involvement; how to *train agency staff to work with women and men at the grassroots*, in a way which allows their voices to be heard and their needs, objectives, and criteria to become central to the project. Quite a lot of dialogue is going on, but it is not being translated into project proposals, where the main voice is usually that of the NGO.

7 Projects do need to have *clear objectives and criteria*, building on knowledge of the roles, responsibilities, and requirements of women and men in the project area. We have to know why we are involved in the projects and what we expect to get out of them, and the people on the ground should also be very clear what they expect out of them. So that if we fail, they can tell us so, and we will know whether we have achieved what we wanted to achieve or not. These things, however, can't be set up in an office, they can't be set up by working through a logical framework from home. It must actually be done together with the people on the ground.

8 Finally, agencies should be far more open in *sharing information*: the findings of their evaluations and the gender-linked issues which they highlight, their experiences of using gender-sensitive models for planning and evaluation, and their experience in generating relevant indicators with both male and female beneficiaries, as well as the indicators they use and find relevant at the agency and funder level.

References

Longwe, Sara (1991), 'Gender awareness: the missing element in the Third World development project', in Tina Wallace and Candida March (eds.): *Changing Perceptions* (Oxford: Oxfam).

Molyneux, Maxine (1985), 'Mobilisation without emancipation? Women's interests, state and revolution in Nicaragua', *Feminist Studies* 11/2.

Moser, Caroline (1991), 'Gender planning in the Third World: meeting practical and strategic needs', in Tina Wallace and Candida March (eds.): *Changing Perceptions* (Oxford: Oxfam).

Overholt, C. *et al.* (1985), *Gender Roles in Development Projects: A Case Book* (West Hartford: Kumarian Press) ('the Harvard Framework').

Gender planning in situations of conflict

Judy El-Bushra, ACORD

ACORD is an operational agency implementing long-term development programmes in Africa. We work at community level: that is, though in certain cases we may undertake specific activities with women, our frame of reference is the community in general. In this presentation I shall first say something about the reasons why we consider that working with women is particularly critical in situations of conflict, and try to identify some of the gaps we have become aware of in our response; and second, give a brief overview of some analytical approaches we have been trying to develop, together with Oxfam, which may help us to build up a more complete picture of women's situation and needs in conflict situations.

In recent years more and more of the areas where ACORD works have been taken over by various forms of turbulence — drought, famine, environmental and economic upheaval, and of course armed conflict, and often several in conjunction — so that now, of the 30-odd programmes operated by ACORD, about two-thirds are either in areas of intense conflict or civil war, or have only very recently emerged from such conflict. We are thus having to accept that in our work emergency situations are becoming the norm rather than the exception, and to make changes to our whole style of working as a result.

The impact of armed conflict upon women

I would first like to consider the sorts of impact that armed conflict has on women in the countries of which I have some knowledge. This is not to argue that conflict is not just as horrific or traumatic for men. (I do not think that is a useful issue to get into.) But it is certainly true that its impact on women is a new issue in the consciousness of planners and policy-makers and hence is not well understood.

Firstly, from the point of view of women's persons, women run very much increased risks of personal violence, especially in those situations of informal, low-level conflict which now appear to be most common. Since women are the ones who are left in villages and who have to leave their houses daily to find food, water, and fuel, they are also the ones who run the risk of being attacked by bandits or caught in the crossfire. The phenomenon of rape as a war weapon has been much publicised in former Yugoslavia, but it is a common one in informal warfare all over the world.

Secondly, communities and families become disrupted in warfare, with women commonly having to take sole responsibility for caring for, protecting, and provisioning the family. They thus have a much heavier work-burden than normal, and this at a time when all types of resource are scarce or non-existent. Agricultural production or livestock-keeping may have to cease if people lose access to their land, or if animals are killed by looters. Gaining a livelihood by selling things in local markets may no longer be an option if one has nothing to sell, or if the marketing system has broken down. Intense difficulties and risks face women in seeking the basic necessities of life, simply because of the absence of services and facilities. Women therefore have to resort to many and various undesirable means of survival for themselves and their families: going without food, entering into unwanted marriages, fleeing to refugee or displaced camps, or taking on socially unacceptable activities such as prostitution.

Attitudes to women's behaviour often become more conservative in wartime. One has the impression that societies undergoing stress look to women as the representatives of cultural continuity and honour, and hence introduce controls — often violent ones — on their movements. At the same time, community structures which make decisions about allocation of resources may exclude women or fail to represent their interests.

Long-term changes to women's lives arising from conflict

In the longer term, a number of changes take place to the division of labour and to family structures as a result of the demographic distortions caused by war. Women start taking on roles in agriculture, for example, that were previously done by men. Sometimes the reverse also happens, but this is much rarer. Both men and women develop different expectations of marriage, and women may find that their 'value' as marriage partners is reduced as their relative numbers increase. These changes are very likely to persist long after the war itself has ended, as has been noted in countries like Cambodia and Uganda, where the impact of war is an important element in understanding gender-relations even now.

An important area of intervention for NGDOs

As this brief overview shows, working to support women in communities overcome by war is vitally important for NGOs that are addressing issues of conflict, if the communities are to have any real chance of survival. In summary, the reasons are three:

• Firstly, the efficiency argument: in the absence of men, women are the main carers, protectors, and providers for their families. Responding to women's needs is therefore probably the most immediate and secure way of protecting the community's vulnerable members.

• Secondly, the ways in which women suffer in war have only recently begun to be recognised, documented, and understood. The brief survey above, for example, has said nothing about the psychological impact of undergoing and witnessing acts of extreme violence, since it is too little understood, and particularly the survey has said nothing of the possible gender-linked differences that might emerge.

• Thirdly, the long-term implications of armed conflict include fundamental and perhaps lasting changes to gender-relations, which have profound implications for the future social and economic health of the community.

How to meet the challenge?

Many barriers face NGOs in rising to this challenge. I would like to mention three in particular.

First, the development of what has been called an 'emergency mentality' among NGOs working in relief and rehabilitation programmes. This syndrome encourages those engaged in relief work to have unrealistically grandiose assumptions about the impact and importance of their role, and suppresses the process of reflection, analysis, and dialogue which should underpin any effective NGO action.

Second, women's needs may not be immediately apparent, owing to their relative 'invisibility' both in the community and to the lack of gender-sensitive attitudes and skills within NGOs. In practice, emergency work frequently ignores both the immediate practical needs of women and their needs for support of a more strategic nature.

Finally, there is a relatively limited conception of what form emergency needs might take. We need to move away from projects focused *a priori* on immediate survival needs such as food and water provision and start considering broader and longer-term needs. These include the need for strengthening the community's own survival mechanisms, the need to maintain self-respect (in matters of personal hygiene and privacy, for example), and the need for psychological support in the aftermath of trauma.

Methods of assessment

I believe that concentrating on methods of assessment offers us one avenue among many for broadening the scope and effectiveness of emergency responses in conflict. Here I draw heavily on work done by Oxfam, in which ACORD also collaborated, on the adaptation of analytical tools for gender work in conflict situations in Asia. The techniques discussed here are analytical frameworks, rather than research methodologies; the adaptation of participatory research methods for use in gender-planning in conflict remains virgin territory. These methods are applicable in evaluation as well as assessment.

The Harvard analytical framework

This framework,[1] developed originally by Harvard University at the request of the US Department of State, has been adapted for a number of other purposes. The adaptation we have used is one developed by UNHCR for use in refugee situations, and this is what I want to talk about here. The Harvard framework is designed to form the basis of a community gender profile, composed of three elements:

• **The gender-determined division of labour:** a list of the respective tasks of men and women, including male and female children. 'Tasks' are grouped in the UNHCR version under four headings: productive activities, reproductive or household activities, social, political, and religious activities, and protection activities.

• **An 'access and control profile':** a list of the resources needed to carry out these tasks. ('Resources' includes material or economic resources, political or social resources, and time.) Then, who has access to these resources (men or women), who has control over their deployment, and who benefits from them?

• **The external factors** which affect the division of labour and the access and control profile of the community.

In the UNHCR version,[2] the community profile is done twice, the first relating to the situation before the flight, the second after it. The second profile indicates not only what the community does and does not have, but also who has lost what and who has gained what. The comparison underlines the fact that a refugee or displaced community is unlikely to be totally destitute: it will have brought with it skills, knowledge, attitudes, values and means of organising itself, even if it has lost all its material resources. Refugee and displaced communities can then be seen as active participants in the solution of their own problems, not as victims whose only option in life is to receive our charity.

This framework has some characteristic elements which we have found particularly useful. These are:

• The importance of resources in relation to responsibilities, and the distinction between access to resources and control over them. We have seen above the importance of women being empowered to take control of the resources they need to carry out their extended family-leadership functions in times of war. We need to know in much more detail how this can happen in particular instances.

• A broad view of what 'resources' means (not just material ones, but also less tangible things like skills and social organisation), and — most importantly for women — time.

• The idea that communities lose some resources over time, but also retain some and gain others. This aspect is particularly important if we are to look seriously at our role in support rather than providing inputs for victims.

Capacities and vulnerabilities

This approach[3] is an extension of some of the ideas behind the Harvard framework, and resulted from a research project carried out by some of the same people, who investigated 41 different NGO projects responding to disasters of different sorts round the world. The underlying conclusion of the study is that, though disasters may strike any community, only in certain communities will a disaster turn into a crisis, beyond the capacity of the community to survive it. The factors which determine the survival ability of a community are:

• Its material and physical assets, such as land, climate, environment, health, skills relating to productive activities, technologies, etc.

• Its social and organisational capacities, including social networks that offer support to people (family, political organisations), systems for distributing goods, services and wealth, etc. Gender issues are critical in this category — societies vary in the extent to which they include or exclude women's participation in such networks.

• Its attitudinal or psycho-social strengths, i.e. whether people feel victimised and dependent, or buoyant and confident. This also is strongly linked to factors of gender.

This framework recognises that different groups within the community (men and women, rich and poor, etc.) will present different profiles, and separate analyses will have to be done if this dynamic is to be properly understood.

The most valuable idea reflected in this framework is the necessity for outside agencies to seek to build on the strengths of the community — before, during, and after a conflict has occurred — to enable it to withstand the effects of conflict with greater internal solidarity. It enables agencies to measure the existing provision of emergency projects against these deep-seated and longer-term requirements.

The Longwe hierarchy of needs

This framework[4] is not specifically relevant to situations of conflict, but may be applied to any situation as a guide to where to focus future activities. What I am presenting here is my own adaptation of the framework to gender planning in the context of ACORD programmes.

The framework looks at the issue of equality of access by men and women to certain key development indicators. They are:

control over resources
participation in decision-making
conscientisation
access to resources
well-being.

These are arranged in a hierarchy, with the bottom one being the focus of initial attention. The framework assumes that the objectives of women's development are ordered according to this hierarchy: thus, equality of control of resources is not truly possible unless equality in the other four spheres has been achieved. Planners can decide where on this grid to place women's condition and position in the community concerned, and resolve to focus on the next line up, albeit bearing in mind that the ultimate goal is complete equality in all aspects.

Discussion

In this short paper it is not possible to enter into a detailed discussion of these different tools. What is important to note is that each one has its advantages and drawbacks, and that these will vary according to circumstances. The trick is to use them in combination, or to continue the work of adapting them. Briefly, the strengths and weaknesses of each are as follows.

The *Harvard Framework* works best when it is looking at detail and when it is being carried out by people who have detailed knowledge of the community. In such a case it can be very informative and give fairly clear and accurate pointers to the most important short-term and long-term needs to be addressed. It insists on bringing into the analysis two factors which are of great importance to women in conflict situations and which are usually overlooked: time as a resource, and women's need for (and roles in relation to) protection. Its weakness, however, is that it is difficult to gain benefit from it if one does not have access to accurate detail. It is also difficult to use across a region or group of communities which may not be totally homogeneous.

The *capacities and vulnerabilities* approach has the potential to generate much insight and understanding of social processes and how communities adapt to crises. The analysis can zoom in on sections of the community or widen out to include the regional or national level. But it offers the temptation to people with a relatively superficial knowledge of the situation to make guesses. And it does not in itself give very clear indications of needs to be addressed.

The *Longwe grid* is a slightly more elaborate version of the Moser practical/strategic dichotomy. But rather than a dichotomy, it presents a progression. It embodies the idea that in women's development, Rome cannot be built in a day, and even apparently basic achievements are worth making. It illustrates quite forcibly what advantages exist in women's situation and what still has to be done. Its disadvantage is that it is static and takes no account of how situations change over time. Some of its basic assumptions (for example the one that the different stages have to be worked through in order) have been questioned.

Conclusion

Confronting issues of gender and conflict requires NGOs to re-examine some of their operational and policy assumptions and give real priority to an analysis of gender-relations and how they are affected by conflict. The aspects of NGO work that need to be examined include gender-policy, policy on emergency work, research and animation methodologies, the need for training staff in new skills such as counselling or conflict resolution, flexibility of approval, and fund-raising mechanisms. The tools of analysis we have looked at here are only one part of that. They oblige us to consider all aspects of a community's life — and women's lives — and not just their needs for food, water, and shelter,which are given so much emphasis in emergency projects.

Notes

1 C. Overholt *et al.* (1985), *Gender Roles in Development Projects: A Case Book* (West Hartford: Kumarian Press).

2 Mary Anderson and the UNHCR Senior Coordinator for Refugee Women (1991), 'A Framework for People-Oriented Planning in Refugee Situations: A Practical Planning Tool for Refugee Workers' (Geneva: UNHCR).

3 Mary Anderson and Peter Woodrow (1989), *Rising From the Ashes: Development Strategies in Times of Disaster* (Boulder, Colorado: Westview Press).

4 Sara Longwe (1991): 'Gender awareness: the missing element in the Third World development project', in Tina Wallace and Candida March (eds.): *Changing Perceptions* (Oxford: Oxfam).

Case studies

The role of policy in mainstreaming gender: the experience of HIVOS

Corina Straatsma

What is HIVOS?

HIVOS is a humanist organisation in the Netherlands, committed to the promotion of human dignity, the right of peoples to self-determination, and the emancipation and empowerment of poor people. It supports a variety of initiatives in the South: people's organisations such as peasant movements, organisations of indigenous people, and women's organisations, human rights programmes, economic activities (credit programmes, cooperatives, agricultural training), and projects concerned with the environment (through private local development organisations — HIVOS has no environmental programmes of its own). There are regional offices in Zimbabwe and India.

WID and the Dutch donor NGDOs

The Dutch donor NGDOs made a relatively late start on integrating WID into their general development policy. There were several reasons for this:

• A prevalence of class ideology: it was argued that, in the struggle for class interests and survival, men and women have equivalent interests, so there was no need for a separate approach to meeting men's and women's needs. The persistence of this view is related to the ideology and approach of partner organisations: their own class-based analysis, or an analysis based on the community, organisation, or family which does not take into account the unequal power relations within households, trade unions, or peasant organisations. These unequal power relations are taken as belonging to the private sphere and therefore not the proper concern of development.

• In the case of indigenous people, gender-relations were held to be defined by culture and therefore not to be touched by Northern interventions.

• A general lack of sensitivity towards gender-related issues such as the different roles and values attributed to women and men, defined by socio-cultural ideas of femininity and masculinity; a fear of feminist ideas.

• Donor organisations are afraid of 'interfering' by discussing sensitive issues like women's development or the transformation of existing gender-linked roles and values.

But perhaps the biggest obstacle of all is simply the lack of adequate information and awareness of gender-relations in relation to culture, and how they affect development projects and limit women's development.

It took a long time for agencies to become aware of the fact that development suffers when women are overlooked. The Nairobi conference played an important role in changing donors' attitude. Agencies discovered the existence of a women's movement in the

In Guatemala HIVOS supports a successful agricultural cooperative in a fairly large Indian community. Although women are active in harvesting crops like coffee, peanuts, and maize, and are engaged in small-scale commerce and handicrafts, they are not members of the cooperative. Their work outside the household is considered 'complementary' to men's work.

While women are passing by, carrying heavy baskets, on their way to market, the male staff of the cooperative tell us how hard it is to find women to join the staff with some knowledge of trade and the ability to do heavy work ...

South, with its own views and ideas, and they realised that it was about time to take account of women's ideas and the way they participate in development.

HIVOS's policy: first steps

HIVOS went through the same process as other Dutch donors. In 1985 we carried out an internal evaluation of the impact on women of development activities funded by HIVOS. The report was an eye-opener, because it tackled the presumed equal interests of poor men and women and the presumed 'gender-neutral' effects of development programmes. It made it clear that women derived scarcely any benefit from training-and-loan programmes and that their interests were not taken into account in project proposals or planning.

After the report we organised several workshops to discuss WID issues and the need for a WID policy. A working group was set up, consisting of representatives of the regional desks, both men and women. Its focus was mainly on WID in the South. At that time we didn't consider it necessary to have an internal WID policy or to have a staff member working on gender-related issues. The group's purpose was to elaborate WID criteria and assess WID policy in the different regions. However, after some time we concluded that criteria and procedures were not enough; what was necessary was an explicit WID policy document with clear goals, to be discussed by all HIVOS staff and partner organisations. There were three motives for this decision:

• **Justice:** women are most oppressed and therefore most deserving of attention.

• **Consistency:** no claim to contribute to the emancipation of poor people can logically overlook women, who are the obvious majority in the poorer strata of society, not only in the South but also the North.

• **Efficiency:** women's contribution to development is essential. Women produce and process food, are engaged in small-scale industry and trade, take care of nearly all the family's needs, and carry a far heavier workload than men. It is mostly because of women's unceasing efforts that poor communities do not collapse. Thus programmes cannot be run efficiently if women are not systematically involved in their preparation and implementation and if their wishes, needs, and interests are not taken into account.

Policy priorities

On this basis we formulated the following policy priorities:

• Working for the social and political empowerment of women through programmes focused on education, facilitating women's participation in decision-making structures, via the formation of women's interest groups and organisations, and networking among like-minded organisations that promote women's interests.

• Promoting women's economic independence through ensuring their access to resources and means of production, as well as control over resources and benefits from their activities.

• The principle that women's right to self-determination regarding their own lives and bodies should be guaranteed and promoted by legal action (e.g. right to abortion, penalisation of all forms of violence against women), sexual education, ensuring women's access to safe and reliable contraception, education of men, etc.

• The elaboration of strategies to lighten women's workload, such as labour-saving techniques, crèches, education of men, etc.

The WID policy document was translated, sent to our partners, and discussed with them, because an active WID policy hinges on good cooperation with local NGDOs. To accelerate this process further, HIVOS decided to increase support to women's organisations, especially those involved in lobbying and influencing public opinion, legislation, and politics.

Evaluation and a new focus on mixed projects

In 1992 we evaluated our policy. We concluded that advances had been made with respect to institutional support of women-only organisations, but that little had been achieved in the case of the so-called 'mixed' organisations. The gender-specific information they provided was still insufficient, and on many occasions

HIVOS had failed to ask for it. We found that WID criteria played a minor role in project approval in the case of mixed organisations.

In order for our WID policy to be more balanced, therefore, we decided to concentrate on the programmes of the mixed NGOs and not to 'delegate' all the responsibility to women-only organisations. For more effective monitoring and assessment in regard to WID, we first analysed the constraints in gender policy and practice faced by NGDOs supported by HIVOS. The study was carried out by means of an analysis of recent external-evaluation documents in which gender issues received special attention, mostly because experts in gender issues were on the evaluation teams.

How NGDOs in the South are dealing with WID issues

As with the donor agencies, discussions on WID and gender in the Southern NGDOs got off to a relatively late start. Attention to WID was seen as inspired by Western feminism; agencies that tackled the issue were accused of donor imperialism; WID was considered to be the latest fashion among donors. Nonetheless, many NGDOs became aware that money was involved, and began to pay lip-service to HIVOS and other donors, stressing the important role of women in development, particularly in their documents.

Also, many women's projects were formulated and set up without any previous gender analysis or feasibility study. There was a boom in income-generating projects (IGPs) for women — poultry-rearing, dress-making, gardening, handicrafts, and the like.

The late 1980s saw a slight change in the attitude of the Southern NGDOs. The destructive effects of war, violence, and structural adjustment hit women harder than men, and NGOs became aware that this had consequences for their programmes. At the same time, the women's movement in many countries was growing stronger, stimulating some openness and awareness of women's issues and gender-relations. Many of our partners started to study the situation of women, organise women's conferences, formulate ambitious targets (for example, that 50 per cent of our loans should go to women), and create separate women's desks. Despite — or perhaps because of — this rapid initial burst, many activities stagnated after a few years: targets were not realised, women lost interest, IGPs failed.

These failures are not difficult to explain. The efforts to integrate women into existing programmes failed in many cases because the activities as such failed to take into account the educational level of women involved, the time they had available, access to the location of the activity, women's specific interests, men's resistance. etc. Also, male fieldworkers, who are common in many NGDOs, may find it difficult to address and motivate women.

The efforts to start separate women's programmes were not always successful, because they presupposed that women have a lot of spare time; they generally did not consider the economic activities which women were already engaged in; there were often problems with marketing, transport, raw-material supply, book-keeping, etc.; they generated very little income; and they failed to challenge existing gender-determined roles.

The provision of budgets and staff was often minimal, as was the support from other teams. Women's programmes tended to be rather isolated in the organisations. The strength of the women's motivation was sometimes overestimated. Women are not always interested in development activities: their interests differ according to their ages, economic situations, relationships with husbands and families. Older women may think that learning new things is reserved for younger generations.

Of course, there are exceptions: women's projects that were successful, both in economic and emancipatory terms. But examples of an integrated approach where women are really considered as equals, with equal access to credit, training, technology, or other services provided by local NGOs, are scarce.

There was a strong connection between progress on gender-aware policy and the composition of staff in the sample of twelve NGOs surveyed. The NGO with the most advanced ideas and activities had an equal number of male and female staff and board members. The NGOs most resistant to WID had female staff only at secretarial level. Moreover, in many organisations female staff continued to be discriminated against in terms of salary, career structures, training, and attendance at seminars.

The contribution of local development NGOs to women's development and empowerment was therefore less than expected, given the NGOs' pretensions to a vanguard role in development, organisation-building, democracy, and the like. It is even probable that this supposed vanguard role has actually *blocked* an open attitude towards men's and women's real interests and preoccupations, and — what is worse — has propagated a paternalistic approach to project planning and people's participation.

The recommendations of the study refer mostly to basic principles of involving both women and men in project planning and organisation for change, listening to them, and making joint analyses and proposals.

Women's organisations: successes and problems

The NGOs in our survey that really made a commitment and a contribution to women's development and the transformation of gender relations were the women-only NGOs, above all those who work from a feminist perspective. They are engaged in a wide variety of activities such as legal aid, action on legal issues and violence against women, reproductive rights, education, leadership training, credit facilitation, organisation-building and so on. Most of these women's NGOs started life as small action groups and evolved into well-staffed and well-organised development NGOs. When they started out, there was a lack of available information — accounts of experiences and successful approaches. This stimulated creativity and inventiveness in methodology, the involvement of women, and action-oriented research. Mixed organisations could have learned from them, but, alas, the interrelation between women-only and mixed NGOs is still problematic in many regions.

Because of hostility towards feminism or feminist issues like reproductive rights or sexual choices, many women's groups tend to focus on strengthening their own organisation and identity rather than trying to influence institutions such as political parties or development NGOs. This inward-looking strategy has not contributed to better mutual understanding. Coordination between women's organisations has also been poor. Their energy is dispersed, often because women with multiple claims on their time can usually give only a limited period to an organisation and tend to leave even leadership positions after a year or so. Despite the concentration on strengthening the organisation, the women's organisations are often institutionally weak. And there is the perennial problem of underfunding.

In spite of all this, however, a growing number of women's organisations are aware of the need to involve mixed organisations, to make alliances, and to get a grasp of politics so as to be able to influence state institutions. There is a growing coordination between women's organisations and state bodies (mainly ministries or departments in charge of women's affairs). On the other hand, the mixed NGOs are also becoming aware that the inequality gap between men and women must be bridged. In these ways, new openings and opportunities are presented — and should be used.

Conclusions

In all this process, donor NGOs have played their part. Both Northern and Southern NGOs not only started late with WID but also made false starts. For our future policy, HIVOS has come to the following conclusions:

• It is important for a donor to have an expressed WID policy with clear goals and criteria and to share this with partner organisations: they have a right to know where you stand and what you want. There should be no hidden agendas. Discussions with partner organisations in workshops or platforms where different experiences are brought together are extremely important for fresh inputs and further development of the policy.

• Don't push partner organisations too hard, or try to condition your support: this leads only to irritation and is counter-productive.

• It is, however, important to be firm and demanding when it comes to information on gender-relations, the impact of the project on women's situation, the impact of women on the project. If details on women's and men's capacities, interests, relationships, access to and control over resources are not available, there is a risk that the existing gap between development opportunities for women and men may be widened even further by your support. If this kind of information is not available or is of poor quality, you should become very suspicious when cultural constraints are mentioned as a barrier to women's participation and development.

• Be firm in the implementation of policy: if an NGO doesn't respond and if women drop further behind through the project activities, stop funding on the grounds of divergence in views. But don't use your purse as a policy instrument in order to change institutions.

• Support for 'sisterhood' (using Sarah Longwe's term) is very important.

• Facilitate gender-training, and monitoring and assessment of gender planning, preferably with the help of local experts.

• Staff training is a necessary (but not sufficient) condition for implementing a gender-aware or WID policy as a donor. Active assessment by the gender-responsible person and regular internal evaluations are also necessary.

• Discuss/question the male/female composition of staff of partner organisations. But note here that if the male/female staff composition or division of labour in your own organisation is unbalanced, it will be difficult to do this and retain credibility.

Staff development and gender training in Oxfam (UK/I)

Bridget Walker

Background: the Gender and Development Unit (GADU)

GADU is one of a number of specialist support units in Oxfam. The Unit was set up in 1985, in response to concern within Oxfam that considerations of gender were not being taken into account in Oxfam policy and programme, and in recognition of the need to mainstream gender in the organisation's work of development, relief, and advocacy.

GADU's history is described elsewhere in detail in this report (see Case Study 3). Its approach to promoting gender-fair practice throughout Oxfam addresses both practical programme support and policy development. To carry both these lines of work forward, it became clear early on that training was a necessary tool, and in 1988 a trainer joined the existing two gender advisers in the unit.

Why training?

Training is not an end in itself. Nor is it the only tool available. It is one of a set of tools for mainstreaming gender in an organisation. Before undertaking a training, therefore, we must ask:

- What is the problem to be addressed?
- Is training the answer?
- What is the desired outcome of the training?
- How is that outcome best achieved?
- How do we measure the success of the exercise?

Training is also a necessary but not a sufficient condition for mainstreaming gender. It must be backed up by policy and procedures for implementation of that policy in practice. Thus, we also need to ask of a training exercise:

- What is the training for?
- Who trains, and with whom?
- When, where, and how is the training carried out?
- After training, what then?

For GADU, these were the important factors:

a. that training should be part of a wider development process;
b. that it should develop or strengthen capacity on the ground;
c. that it should be 'custom-made' for Oxfam, providing a consistent approach which could be replicated, but was also flexible and adaptable according to circumstances and needs;
d. that training would be directed primarily at Oxfam's own staff;
e. that it should make the most effective use of limited resources.

Training is a transformative process: it aims to increase knowledge, to develop understanding, to change behaviour, and to offer new skills with which to do this. The relationship between knowledge and behaviour is intricate: effecting a change in work practices can lead to a change in understanding (as well as the reverse). But training does not lead in itself to change in attitude as such — although some trainers would argue that this, too, should be the aim in the case of gender training.

What is gender training?

We see gender training as existing on a spectrum. At one end is gender-planning training, involving the use of analyses such as the Harvard framework, and the models of Moser and Levy, in order to analyse project plans and to plan from a gender-based perspective. Training of this kind is often aimed at decision-makers, such as officials in development ministries, and tends to be top-down and non-participatory in its mode of address. Used in this way it can become a mechanistic tool; for example, the use of the terminology of gender planning such as 'equity' and 'empowerment' may not be grounded in the principles of gender-fair development.

At the other end of the spectrum is awareness-raising, building on the insights and methods of the women's movement. It is more experiential and participatory, and typically begins from personal issues and leads outwards to the political.

Oxfam's training is a combination of these. It includes planning, relating directly to Oxfam's programmes; but it is also experiential and flexible, aiming to take account of the different contexts of our work.

It should be kept in mind that the training described here is designed primarily for Oxfam staff, but it may also address issues of how to raise concerns about gender with partner organisations. Oxfam field staff also carry out a wide range of gender-related training activities with partner organisations.

Training offered by GADU

In the UK and Ireland, GADU has organised courses for staff in the Overseas Division, focusing particularly on managers, with a special session for overseas managers who come to Oxfam House for a management-induction course. New work is being developed on a thematic basis, and there have been workshops on gender and emergencies and conflict, to assist staff to incorporate a gender-based perspective into their work on disaster response and relief (see Thematic Paper 3).

For Oxfam staff generally there is a Gender and Development course, which provides a basic introduction to the issues. Then there is a focus on gender in Oxfam's communications policy and practice in the development education and advocacy structures in Oxfam. Like the Gender and Development course, the Gender and Communications course is open to all Oxfam staff.

A three-day Knowledge of Oxfam course is part of the induction of all new staff, and this includes a session on gender as one of a number of options. GADU is responsible for this session.

Oxfam's Training Department runs an Equal Opportunities training course and a course on recruitment and selection. These include gender-related components. The first is mandatory for all staff, and all managers involved in staff recruitment must attend the second. By contrast, gender-training courses are voluntary or are designed by special request and agreement with the departments concerned.

Overseas, there are various kinds of training.

• *At regional level*: the gender training which took place in Chad in January 1992 is an example of a process that has happened in a number of regions. The staff in Oxfam's offices in francophone West Africa initially put gender on the agenda of a regional meeting. This was followed by a regional seminar on the issue, from which a recommendation and request came to GADU for gender training. The training itself was a five-day workshop for managers and programme staff from the region. To date, training has always been by request, not imposed on staff in the field.

• *At country level*: where possible, gender training has been carried out at a regional level, thus maximising resources and enabling exchange of information and experience between different country programmes However, there are some instances where it has been appropriate to undertake training at country level, for example in Ethiopia, where there is a large staff, engaged not only in funding support of partner organisations but also in running a number of operational programmes, particularly of a relief and rehabilitation nature.

• *As part of a network*: at about the same time as GADU was set up, AGRA (Action for Gender Relations in Asia) was established as a network concerned with gender issues in programme work in Asia. Most of the Asia training has taken place within the context of network meetings, often around a particular theme. AGRA is now divided into two different geographical sections; the most recent AGRA East meeting, held in Thailand in 1993, had conflict as its central theme.

• *Training for trainers*: a workshop was carried out in India in 1991. It included partner organisations and examined training methodologies in the context of gender-related issues.

• *Thematic training*: the example of conflict has been given above. Another theme on which both GADU and other Oxfam staff have held workshops is the gender-related aspects of income generation.

• *Focus on a specific sector*: an example here is a workshop on fisherfolk held in the Philippines.

• *Training run jointly with others*: in 1992 the Oxfam Emergencies Unit ran a training workshop in Delhi for Oxfam staff in Asia concerned with emergency response. GADU was invited to contribute to the planning of the workshop; this included integrating considerations of gender into such areas as emergency assessment, and there was also a half-day session specifically on applying gender-based perspectives to emergency response.

• *Preparatory work with other colleagues* for their own training sessions, such as discussions with the Oxfam Technical Unit prior to their training workshop on water provision. GADU did not participate in the training, but contributed to the planning and resources.

Outside Oxfam, when the EC/NGO network in the UK decided to look at gender training, Oxfam was instrumental in designing the first of a series of workshops for member agencies.

For emergency work Oxfam sometimes uses consultants who are available at short notice. Unlike Oxfam staff they may have had no exposure to gender concerns. In 1993, therefore, GADU participated in a training workshop organised by Red R (Register of Engineers for Disaster Relief), and highlighted the needs of refugee and displaced women.

Methods

GADU's training is located in practical experience in many countries, of women's roles and relationships, the cultural, social, and political context in which those roles and relationships exist, and also the historical context, customs, and traditions.

We regard gender-aware and gender-fair development as the responsibility of both women and men. Training must therefore involve both (although there is also a place for work with separate groups of women), as men need to take on responsibility for work on gender and need to know how to do it. In our training workshops GADU always works with co-facilitators from the region, male as well as female where possible.

What this training aims to do is to offer some tools for analysis of the different roles and situations of women and men in development. These tools may include learning about and applying the different methodologies to our own programme, planning, assessing, monitoring, and evaluation from a gender-based perspective. Questions covered may include:

- how to gather and use baseline data;
- the importance of disaggregated data;
- how to listen to women and work with them;
- how to raise issues with partner organisations;
- how to communicate gender-related issues;
- how to give thematic work, such as emergencies, or work on debt, a gender dimension.

It is very important to document the training subsequently, as a guide for future learning.

GADU is currently working on the recording and consolidation of Oxfam's experience of gender training. We have commissioned the production of a gender-training manual, which we hope will incorporate learning from both the South and the North. Work has also been done on the development of guidelines for managers within the organisation.

Impact

We have found that gender training does have a notable impact, and a training session or workshop is often a memorable event with very positive results. Training is a valuable team-building exercise. It can — and often does — lead to increased awareness of gender-linked issues and needs. It is not easy to measure the impact of training, because there are so many other variables, but the resultant outputs may be seen as possible indicators. This can include, for example, a country team deciding to write or revise policy for its own programme, the inclusion of gender issues in project criteria, the setting of minimum standards, the application of gender-awareness to planning and evaluation exercises, and work with partner organisations to raise and address gender-related issues. Gender-awareness may be applied in a new situation; for example, in the recent drought in Southern Africa the Oxfam team in Zambia applied principles of gender-aware work to their response to the disaster. This ensured that women had a major say in the relief programmes developed and contrasts with the 'service delivery' style that has often been a characteristic of emergency responses.

At a less immediately practical level, gender training has thrown up a range of theoretical and strategic issues and provided a forum for analysis and discussion of what exactly we mean by 'development'. The examination of unequal roles and power structures raises issues about the distribution of power between the centre and the periphery, and North/South relations in general and in Oxfam's relation to its partners and regional staff. It can highlight common defence/avoidance strategies, such as labelling gender a 'cultural imposition'. On the other hand it has also been described as a post-feminist concept, co-opting the insights of the women's movements rather than supporting the feminist demand for change and social justice

Gender training also makes people look critically at the work-culture of the organisation and at Oxfam as an institution where gender policy is formally approved, but there is a long way to go in practice, for instance in recruitment. It highlights other areas of need for staff development, such as further training skills. The methodology presents models of ways of working which are more participatory, and can be a democratising process.

Thus, GADU's experience of gender training has confirmed that it does provide a perspective and a set of tools for approaching an analysis of social and gender-determined roles and relationships.

Some problems and difficulties

All this is not to say that there have been no difficulties. Certain difficulties are specific to Oxfam's structure; for instance, GADU's position in the Overseas Division has resulted in some difficulties in addressing cross-divisional issues and responsibilities such as recruitment. Since equal opportunities work has been addressed in a different Oxfam Division, it is not always integrated with GADU's work, and although there has been a link through the person of the trainer, the conceptual links need to be made much stronger. There is a need to understand both the common strands between the two areas and their distinctive differences. The issue of equal opportunities in recruitment and selection needs to be seen not only as a procedure which is enabling for women candidates, but also as a procedure which tests the levels of awareness of social and gender-linked issues in candidates and in the organisation at large. A tactic to achieve this could be to carry out training side by side with equal opportunities work on job descriptions.

In fact, there seems to be a kind of 'either/or' treatment of gender and equal opportunities issues. Oxfam's equal opportunities policy was a significant factor in getting a gender policy on the agenda; but that policy has now been approved at a moment when the equal opportunities policy seems weak. Opportunities for mutually reinforcing both policies should not be missed.

Also specific to Oxfam is the advisory nature of GADU, even within the Overseas Division. This has been problematic in ensuring that good practice actually happens. The three-cornered contract between participant, trainer, and manager has been weak, because the implementation of gender-aware or gender-fair programmes has not been a management responsibility. It is hoped that this will change radically with the organisation's adoption of the gender policy for the whole of Oxfam, with a clear message from senior management that it is the responsibility of managers and not GADU to 'police' that policy. The most pressing need is probably for the training of managers. Gender training itself has never been mandatory in the majority of the work we have done; thus it is often the case that, while those in the field have received training, the manager back at Oxfam House may not have done so.

Another constraint is the problem of chronic under-resourcing. This is certainly the case in Oxfam, but equally certainly is something common to all work on women.

There is also the problem that gender training may be seen as a panacea. As we noted at the outset, gender training is a tool, one of many, and cannot deal with all the weaknesses of a programme. At the level of staffing, for example, in some teams there is still a serious shortage of women in senior positions; the work culture may not be supportive to women; there may be no clearly defined policy for staff development. At the level of procedures the advice on gender may not be implemented: for example, the questions on the Project Application Summary Form relating to the position of women in the project may be left unanswered, data are not disaggregated by gender, and it is therefore difficult to ascertain how gender-linked concerns are being addressed in practice.

Finally, there is a need for consistency across all areas of Oxfam's work. Advocacy, relief, and development all need to be approached from a gender-based perspective.

Conclusions

The following is a (non-exhaustive) list of the lessons GADU has learned from its training experience:

• Training is most effective when it is part of an integrated approach to gender, within a clear policy framework and with management commitment to implementation.

• The expectations of training may be unrealistic, especially if the training is not followed up. A one-off workshop will have little impact without follow-up, which should therefore be written into the original training programme. Follow-up should include specific objectives, a timetable for implementation, identification of those responsible, and procedures for review of progress.

• Training is part of a process. As such, its objectives within the process need to be clear.

• Networks provide a supportive environment for the development of training. Sharing information and experiences of is useful and mutually enriching.

• We must keep in mind that gender issues are complex and sensitive, breaking new ground for many people and tackling old, entrenched habits of thought and action. Thus training can be seen as both threat and promise by different participants. Strong reactions are to be expected.

• While it is important that both women and men do gender training, they have different expectations and understandings of it, and different needs for either support or challenge and questioning.

• Finally, gender training itself is in a constant process of development as a result of experience. There is still much to learn!

References

Moser, Caroline O. N. (1991), 'Gender planning in the Third World: meeting practical and strategic gender needs', in Tina Wallace and Candida March (eds.): *Changing Perceptions.* Oxford: Oxfam Publications.

Moser, Caroline O.N. and Caren Levy (1986), *A Theory and Methodology of Gender Planning: Meeting Women's Practical and Strategic Needs*, DPU (Development Planning Unit) Gender and Planning Workshop Paper no. 11, London.

GADU: a specialist gender unit in Oxfam (UK/I)

Eugenia Piza-López

The experience of the Gender and Development Unit of Oxfam (UK and Ireland) is rich and varied. There have been successes and difficulties; and it would be impossible to cover the whole range of experiences in a single case study. In this paper I shall focus on the strengths and weaknesses of having a separate unit as a structure to promote gender-fair practice in Oxfam. Although I want to concentrate on the difficulties and challenges, in the hope that others can learn from our mistakes, this should not obscure Oxfam's very considerable achievements in the field of gender and development.

It should be said at the outset that the debate on the best structures to promote gender-fair practice in NGDOs should not be limited to whether to create a separate unit with specialist staff or integrate it into everybody's job. Gender work does not take place in an institutional vacuum, and the nature and functioning of each institution will determine its potential for change, areas of blockage, and potential allies. Thus, for each NGDO, its structure, institutional culture, and ways of working should be decisive in selecting the best approach or structure for its gender work.

The potential and difficulties of integrating gender described in this case study correspond to a relatively large agency with staff on the ground operating in many countries and cultures on a wide range of development activities: education, lobbying, fundraising, relief, and development.

Oxfam and the creation of GADU

Oxfam's work in development and relief in over 72 countries is managed from 45 field offices. Field representatives have decision-making powers for programme and policy development, staffing (including specialist staff), and management within agreed policy. Many field offices have or have had gender specialists. In the UK and Ireland the structure includes regional desks, advisory units, of which GADU is one, and departments, plus area offices responsible for fundraising, education, and campaigning.

GADU was formally created in 1985 by the Overseas Director as an advisory unit for Oxfam's programme, with one part-time worker. Since 1988 there have been four staff members on open-ended contracts and two or three on fixed-term contracts responsible for special projects. We also work with consultants.

GADU's work has expanded progressively from its original focus on projects and programmes overseas (1985-89) to include the UK and Ireland operations (campaigning, fundraising, information) and lobbying (1989/90 to the present). Our mandate is to integrate a concern for gender into all aspects of Oxfam's programme: policy development, programme advice, training, and lobbying. Within this remit our broad aims have been:

- to establish gender as a legitimate development discipline and field of expertise within Oxfam;

- to create awareness of gender as a development issue and a perspective that contributes to sound practice;

- to provide a bridge between development practitioners, academics and activists in the North and the South;

- to promote a shift in programmes to ensure that women are consulted and their specific needs as women met;

- to scale up the programmes by lobbying bilateral and multilateral aid donors.

Various strategies to address all areas of Oxfam's work have been developed. These have included:

- internal lobbying for changes and allocation of resources to gender work;

- training to promote cultural change;

- constantly raising questions of best practice, direction, and the politics of aid, from our standpoint as a unit;

- using a mixture of 'soft' and 'hard' styles in internal communication;

- using gender-focused external networks for support, learning and solidarity-building.

Institutional obstacles to the promotion of gender

Broadly, the main obstacles to the integration of gender-fair policies into Oxfam's programme result from two factors: the institution's own structural limitations, and the problems intrinsic in constructing an agenda for gender-fair social change in patriarchal societies.

Problems resulting from Oxfam's structure

One source of difficulty is the advisers' low status within the organisation. For instance, programme-support services such as GADU have only an advisory function. They do not hold budgets and they do not have decision-making power. Also, the location of the gender unit in Oxfam's UK headquarters gives rise to tensions between staff at the centre and staff at the periphery, hindering acceptance of the Unit's advice; and the predominant emphasis on geopolitical rather than thematic work has made it difficult to work on cross-cultural issues.

Oxfam's prevailing management style also militates against effective integration of gender-fair policies: it has been relatively loose and is effectively decentralised. Organisational backing for the imposition of structures and procedures and the setting of standards is lacking, with the result that these things are done only on a voluntary basis. Field staff are on four-year fixed-term contracts, and staff turnover is high.

All these factors mean that support services have had to work where they were given access and could create alliances. Their position in these conditions has been fragile and vulnerable to changes in staffing.

Problems resulting from gender issues themselves

An obstacle often raised to the integration of gender issues into mainstream development policy is the argument about the sanctity of 'culture' and the dangers of interventionism — another facet of the tensions between the centre and the periphery. This also links into a development analysis which, until recently, emphasised class and ethnicity at the expense of gender.

The personal and the professional have tended to overlap when addressing gender issues. The conventional view of gender specialists is that they are pursuing their personal agendas as women in arguing for gender-sensitive policies and practice. This bolsters resistance to gender issues from both men and women.

Finally, consensus has been lacking on the relative importance of gender, and there has been unwillingness to examine the issues involved. Until recently gender issues were taken on board largely by committed individuals in the UK and overseas, and therefore the continuity and funding of the work was vulnerable to staff changes. This was not helped by the shortage of women in senior management positions.

This latter constraint made a secure institutional framework for gender work in Oxfam essential. However, a concern with a 'bottom-up' policy-development strategy which developed and emerged from our programme meant that the unit's work for some years was not securely positioned within the organisation. Policy work started in 1987, both in the field and the UK. Oxfam's gender policy was finally approved by Council in May 1993 after extensive consultation.

Dismantling the obstacles

Promoting social change in a large organisation and facing the difficulties outlined above has been a challenging task. GADU has combined three strategies to put the issues on the agenda and change working practice and culture:

- a multi-pronged approach, working at the levels of programmes, policy, and advocacy;
- building strategic alliances;
- promoting management support for institutionalisation.

A multi-pronged approach

The unit's main activities are varied, and include policy development, programme support and advice, training, resources and communications, lobbying and networking, and organisational culture. These areas of work have been developed and refined over the years. Sometimes it has been a planned process; sometimes it has resulted from institutional coincidences.

Work on *policy and procedures* has been slow and painstaking, directed towards developing a gender policy and mainstreaming gender into existing procedures, sometimes working with allies, sometimes striving to influence managers. GADU has tried to ensure the integration of gender-fair policies into development, relief, and personnel procedures, by participating in recruitment and selection, raising the issues, requesting more gender-aware managers. In 1992, when the Overseas Division was restructured, gender-awareness was included in all new job descriptions for managers, and this is increasingly becoming a criterion in the selection process.

Programme-support activities have included field trips, in-house project appraisal, monitoring and evaluation. This has had a gradual and significant impact in improving the integration of

Turning a project around: the Wello water project

In an Oxfam-supported project to assist in the improvement and provision of water supplies, wells were installed in many communities and springs were protected. The objective was to work through existing channels, including government administrators and local leaders such as the farmers' association chairman.

Problems with the pumps started to emerge, including technical faults and difficulties encountered by women users. When concerns were raised about consultation with women as users, Oxfam went back to the community and assessed the gender-dimension of the project. As a result it was decided to construct open wells and strengthen community participation in project management. A liaison team of four women was set up and a Community Participation Officer was appointed. She worked alongside engineers in design and consultation.

gender issues into programmes and projects and in reaching out for new partners working on the issues.

As part of *training* on planning and awareness-building (see Case Study 2), field offices in Asia, Latin America, and Africa organised regional meetings for staff to debate gender issues. These meetings overcame GADU's isolation from the overseas offices and created a base of support. It also enabled GADU staff to develop a working definition of gender which reflected cultural diversity.

Complex and challenging discussions have taken place on an on-going basis on many issues, ranging from 'what is gender?' to how to raise issues with partners, how to work where there are no NGOs, how to reach women in highly centralised societies, and the role of income-generation projects in promoting women's mobility. The level of debate varies widely between field offices, but very many have tried to come to terms with concerns about gender and relate them to their work. GADU has been very involved in this process.

Institutional learning has been promoted through publications and internal newsletters, development seminars, a specialist library, issue-based meetings, and feedback into Oxfam's publications. Especially in the 1985-7 period and in 1993, the unit raised many questions in relation to Oxfam's *institutional culture* and the position and needs of women in the labour force. When GADU was created, it successfully campaigned with staff in the equal opportunities and women's groups for a crèche for the children of staff at Oxfam's headquarters.

AGRA South and AGRA East

Action for Gender Relations in Asia (AGRA) is a network of Oxfam staff in the region aimed at promoting awareness and integrating gender issues into programme. Set up in 1985 as a forum for female staff, it gradually came to involve men and women. Among its activities AGRA has undertaken extensive training in awareness building for all programme and administrative staff, including drivers. Project reviews and staff exchanges have also taken place. Today the network is divided into East and South, and meetings continue to take place on a thematic basis. In 1993 there were workshops on gender and employment and gender and armed conflict.

Raising gender issues in the workplace enabled the unit to make links with women at different levels and work with committed staff on meeting gender-needs in the organisation. However, the need to have an impact on programme work, together with limited resources, led to prioritisation of the overseas programme for some years, during which the unit was not sufficiently in touch with staffing issues and female staff.

Creating strategic alliances

Central to GADU's achievements has been the existence of gender-specialist staff and gender-sensitive female country representatives based in the field offices. They have acted as catalysts for gender work: networking with grassroots women and women's organisations, promoting policy development and training of partners, and, for instance in Asia, creating staff networks on gender. These staff were, and continue to be, key allies in promoting links between the unit and the field. Many of the difficulties faced by gender specialists in the field are similar to those of GADU. However, this *ad hoc* network has been instrumental in carrying forward concerns for gender-fair development.

Again because of limited resources, GADU prioritised work with these staff when strategising support to the programme, as a way to learn from the programme and root the unit's perspectives and activities in Oxfam's experience. Programmes with gender specialists and those open to work on gender issues were given inputs and support. This enabled GADU to implement its objectives. However, it must be kept in mind that creating alliances and working through them is a dynamic process, and also a negotiating process where mistakes can be made. GADU has had to change its approach and style to response to structures and concerns in the field.

A similar strategy has taken place at headquarters, where GADU has developed joint efforts with some departments and units to take forward gender-related issues and has linked its lobbying initiatives to UK-based networks.

GADU now considers working with allies a strategic approach to the promotion of gender and to working in ways that reflect a developmental approach. However, the work would be fragile and unsustainable without an institutional framework and management support.

Oxfam's strategic objectives for its programme on gender, 1992-5

Aim: To make gender analysis and response integral to the whole of Oxfam's programme in emergencies, development, and communications, and ensure that Oxfam is proactive and influential on gender issues.

Objectives:

1 to agree and implement a gender policy for Oxfam;

2 to incorporate gender-awareness into recruitment and selection in the Overseas and Marketing Divisions and other personnel procedures and practice, and into management induction and staff development;

3 to enable staff to assess, monitor, and evaluate work from a gender-based perspective and to achieve acceptable standards for implementation;

4 to make managers accountable for improved performance in incorporating a gender-based perspective into the work for which they are responsible, whether in development, emergencies, or communications/advocacy;

5 to promote appropriate gender policies in other donor bodies and raise the level of public debate on gender;

6 to implement a contract with the Marketing Division in order to ensure that gender concerns are fully integrated into Oxfam's communications work.

GADU has recently initiated a linking project with an emphasis on staff meeting and learning from each other (see Case Study 9a). The project, which has a two-year life span, includes regional consultation with partners and women's organisations on key development issues, and extensive work by field offices in reviewing their programme and preparing issue-based case studies to distil best practice.

Institutionalising gender through management support

Since 1992, the climate for gender work in Oxfam has changed. The concept of gender-fair development has gained legitimacy and it forms an important part of programme plans and priorities. The key to this change has been the support of senior managers, especially gender-sensitive women, and their commitment to taking gender issues forward at corporate level. A policy has now been agreed. This has provided a framework for monitoring and implementation, and will continue to do so.

Managers at all levels are now responsible and accountable for policy implementation. This may bring significant changes in Oxfam's programme and working culture. This process has ensured the integration of gender-based concerns in the Strategic Plan for Oxfam's programme overseas and in the Strategic Intent for Oxfam as an institution.

Conclusion

GADU's experience, like that of many other NGDOs, illustrates that there is no infallible recipe for integrating gender-fair practice into all aspects of the institution and its work. We have learned three major lessons from our approach:

• It is important to work on policy development from the start, in order to enable gender specialists and managers to have a guiding framework for the work and to achieve sustainable changes.

• The process of work on policy development can be incorporated as part of a strategy of awareness-building and raising of issues, and should be participatory.

• It is better to combine work on programme issues with work on gender issues in the workplace, both to strengthen female staff throughout the organisation and to promote working cultures consistent with programme policy.

Structures to promote gender within MS

Gitte Berg

What is MS?

MS (Danish Association for International Cooperation) works in the following areas:

- development in the South;
- international understanding;
- solidarity;
- information/education in the North through development work in the South;
- cross-cultural solidarity (e.g. with immigrants, refugees).

MS operates in ten countries, mostly in Africa, and also has offices in Central America and Nepal.

Within a general overall objective of poverty alleviation, women comprise one of the four priorities chosen by MS as objectives for its development cooperation efforts. The other three priority areas are development by people, the environment, and sustainability.

MS has had an explicit policy on women and gender written into its official documents since 1981, requiring that women and men are provided with equal opportunities and access to resources and benefits, decision-making and power, with an emphasis on development by people.

Gender policy in MS: a history

Since 1975 (the date of our first women's conference), groups of women in MS have been working on a women's policy and development with women. First there was an informal MS women's group, which is still operating, and later a more formal women's policy committee was established. Since 1989 MS has employed a full-time women's consultant.

The 'accompanying spouse' clause introduced to our staff-recruitment policy in 1977 resulted in work with women's activities and women's groups, initially informally via so-called 'non-requested development workers'. This work has developed into specific, requested women's activities. At first these were undertaken mostly from a welfare and anti-poverty perspective, for instance by means of income-generating projects. This approach has now changed and a greater emphasis is put on the productive role and empowerment of women.

These were some milestones in the 1980s and early 1990s in progress towards the concretisation of MS's gender policy and the creation of structures in the organisation to support it:

• In 1981 the MS task force on women published a 'White Paper' which laid the formal foundation for future work, giving higher priority to women in development.

• A report published in 1989 by the Danish anthropologist Rie Odgaard, entitled *How do African women benefit from the volunteer aid programme?*, provided the final argument justifying the creation of a women's consultant post.

• In 1991, the MS programme in Zimbabwe carried out a study entitled *Hello, is gender there?*, written by Ellen Farr and Rudo Chitiga.

• Finally, *Half and half: guidelines for development cooperation with women* was published in early 1993, as the official policy document in MS, approved by the political system. These guidelines are the fruit of a process of three years' work, involving Danish development workers and staff in the South and in Denmark and a four-person working group. Over the next two years (from 1993), *Half and half* will be integrated as policy in MS Denmark and MS in the South.

Problems and constraints

MS thus has a written, officially approved policy on gender-fair development, forged over many years of work. However, difficulties arise with implementation, even though people working on gender in MS have developed or recommended various tools to raise gender-awareness in the organisation: gender-sensitive recruitment, gender training, project manuals, evaluations, etc.

Why do these difficulties occur? Partly, because gender and the implications of a gender analysis for agency practice in all areas are still not fully understood by everyone in the organisation; but also because the structure of a 'normal' organisation, MS included, often operates as a system of constructed inequality and marginalisation in which gender consultants or other people working on gender have unequal access to status, power, the setting of agendas, and the making of decisions.

This imbalance has come about partly because MS's women and gender policy was integrated at a late stage in a process initiated as long ago as 1975, with the employment of a women's consultant in 1989; and partly because the gender issue is not regarded as sacrosanct, unlike other development issues such as environment and people-centred development.

There are two basic elements in the policy on women which inevitably provoke resistance at all stages:

- it promotes equal opportunities and women's empowerment;
- it challenges male power by potentially undermining management's accepted values and by cutting across settled hierarchies.

As with any new policy, the introduction of a gender policy will always arouse resistance: the need for it will be questioned, it will be opposed for 'technical' reasons, it will be labelled a 'political' issue because it contradicts or displaces a previous policy. Indeed the introduction of policy — and particularly gender policy — is a highly political undertaking. Moreover, gender issues confront the political and the personal in a way that forces women and men to reflect on relationships in their own lives as well as the larger patterns of gender-relations. Women may be seen as 'too aggressive' and men may feel the need to defend their own gender-determined roles. At the broader level, ideas about gender are not just about men and women, but also subvert the whole way in which organisations are run. If gender-fair policies are fully integrated into an organisation, they change ways of working, impose more complex analyses (ones that include feelings, for example), and enforce a new dialogue between women and men. In structural terms, resistance is closely allied with problems of top-down management structures at various points: within the organisation; from North to South; and within partner organisations.

So how do we 'sell' the gender policy to the organisation? There are a number of important constraints. The main constraint is a general one concerned with the hierarchisation of development objectives. In most organisations, other policies, such as poverty alleviation and counteracting inequalities due to class or racial differences, are treated as the primary development objectives. In this schema the unequal position of women and legalised discrimination against women are subsumed. Women's unequal situation is also regarded as an 'internal matter' in the countries and cultures of the South, in which we have no right to interfere. Among other problems, this view is based on an erroneous perception of 'culture' as something static and unchanging.

There is also a constraint related to different levels of understanding in different areas of the organisation. In overseas programmes, and with overseas development workers, MS gender staff talk in terms of 'women', because people have difficulty understanding 'gender' or the distinction between WID and GAD. At home, however, in development education work, they do talk in terms of 'gender', for example in discussing how to get women's views and values on issues of trade and debt into development education. This is a strategic choice. The additional input into discussions of trade and debt obtained by adding a gender-based perspective can make development education on these macro-economic issues more interesting by 'humanising' them.

Strategies for enforcing implementation of the gender policy

Gender specialists in MS have recognised, therefore, that careful strategies have to be sought for getting a gender policy implemented. These strategies need to be targeted on two levels:

• *management and leadership*: responsibility for gender-fair practices must be written into the organisation's power structure, and management should be accountable in this regard;

• *dialogue* in daily working life: this involves networking, communication with activists, desk officers, etc., to make sure that knowledge of gender issues percolates through the organisation.

More specifically, the strategy involves:

• Integrating gender within the organisational structure. Restructuring in MS has recently been carried out to incorporate structures responsible for gender work.

• Making gender-awareness and a gender-analysis methodology a key tool and professional qualification for programme staff in the Danish and Southern offices of MS. To be effective in practice, this depends on the new structure.

• Making gender-linked concerns an integral part of all development work and policy in MS Denmark. This requires planned training of management and key people at the top levels of the organisation.

• Mainstreaming and agenda-setting.

• On-going monitoring. Two country programmes are being reviewed each year and gender-fair methodology is being incorporated into terms of reference, review guidelines, and team composition. Policy papers are produced every second year, and there are annual reports.

• Networking and lobbying to promote continuous dialogue on gender throughout the organisation. This needs suitable resource people. The task force in this respect is the Women and Gender Policy working group.

The gender unit or gender consultant

MS's gender consultant will in future be working more closely with the head of MS and with management. However, the job of the gender consultant is to be a resource, a catalyst, and a lobbyist. She has competence but not responsibility for integrating gender throughout the organisation — that is the job of management. The tasks of the gender consultant (or gender unit) include:

- raising the issue of gender and lobbying on it within all areas of the organisation;
- coordinating and networking;
- introducing the gender-analysis and encouraging gender-awareness via training;
- introducing methodologies for implementing policy on gender and women in the organisation;
- developing and introducing tools, mechanisms and procedures for monitoring and evaluating the gender policy.

Finally, it should be recognised that gender is a professional specialism, and the gender unit in an NGDO — whatever form it takes — is a specialist structure. Gender-awareness and a gender-analysis are therefore part of the professional qualifications for the gender staff, and a requirement of the job.

This has important consequences for staff recruitment and selection procedures; contracting and terms of contracts; renewal or otherwise of contracts preceding the introduction of gender policy; and the selection of trainers if not in-house. However, only the heads of department or other senior managers can ensure this and have the power to enforce the fulfilment of requirements and conditions.

A gender unit or officer, or integration of gender into all structures in the organisation?

We have found that in order to achieve full integration of gender into the organisation, special provisions and personnel are necessary. There is a contradiction at policy level between a gender policy calling for mainstreaming and an emphasis on gender as a specific area. This will only be resolved, and our gender policy satisfactorily integrated into the structure of the organisation, if there is both acknowledged responsibility at management level for integration of the gender perspective throughout the organisation, side by side with a 'special desk officer' for women, a gender consultant, and a task force for gender policy.

North/South dialogue: the experience of Novib

Adrie Papma

Novib's history of dialogue with partner organisations in the South on the integration of gender-fair practice is over ten years old. Over that period we have concluded that it is very difficult to have a direct influence on partners' policy on gender. For this to happen, various support structures and mechanisms in the South are necessary. Novib has been developing work in the promotion of such structures since the mid-1980s. This method of working has in turn influenced Novib's policy and led to changes within the agency itself. Women's organisations, particularly from Latin America, have challenged Novib's relations with its partners.

Gender policies aimed at the empowerment of women are a crucial element of Novib's ultimate objective of alleviating structural poverty. The basic elements of our gender policy towards partners are:

- providing institutional support on gender-related concerns to both mixed and women's organisations;
- promoting support platforms, thematic working groups, and networks for partner/partner relations and exchanges;
- investing in local consultants to accompany partners in developing their own gender policy and practice;
- working towards more equal relations between partners and donor organisations via South/North project linkages and networks.

Some elements in Novib's strategy are described below.

Developing a gender policy in partner organisations

Novib encourages the development of gender-fair policies within partner organisations. Here we operate at two levels: first, in promoting a gender policy within all partner organisations; and second, in supporting autonomous women's organisations, both at the level of the target group — to provide poor women with increased access to and control over resources and decision-making — and the level of political claim-making — to foster the development of ideas and strategies for addressing more structural dimensions of women's subordination.

Currently, Novib supports 85 women's organisations — about 10 per cent of all Novib partners. A new strategy is to encourage women's organisations to build working relations with mixed organisations and institutions, with the objective of promoting cooperation and the formulation and implementation of a gender policy among mixed organisations. For instance, together with the Dutch Overseas Cooperation Ministry, Novib has recently carried out an evaluation of the relationships between NGDOs and women's centres in Peru and Colombia (results forthcoming).

A problem we have encountered in encouraging the formulation of a gender-fair policy among partners is that of phasing the process: should all the partners be formulating policy at once, or in series, beginning with the most gender-sensitive — or the most resistant? This is both a tactical problem, in terms of developing a pool of knowledge among partners, and a problem of capacity for Novib and for local consultants.

NGO platforms

These platforms grew out of *policy platforms*, which were organised as a mechanism to increase and organise consultation processes after Novib was criticised by partners for unilateralism in its policy definition in the 1980s. The policy platforms grew into local, national, or regional platforms or networks of NGOs, including some that were not within Novib's sphere of influence.

Concurrently with this development, the decision was taken in Novib to make gender and development one of its main lines of action. Thus the country and regional platforms, at which Novib partner organisations formulate recommendations for Novib's country-specific policy, are important forums at which mixed organisations and women's organisations can discuss GAD issues. On the platforms also a space has been created for women's organisations to meet with senior representatives of mixed organisations.

Use of local consultants

Local independent consultants provide long-term institutional support to partner organisations in their work on gender. Consultants play an important role in the dialogue between Novib and its partners. However, consultants are not an intermediary link between partners and Novib, and do not participate in decision-making on programmes and projects. The relationship is triangular: a local, independent consultant may be hired by the partner, by Novib, or by both.

Novib is compiling two pools of consultants with different skills and orientations. One group are experts on gender and development: these play an important role in accompanying partners, mainly mixed NGOs, in their processes of formulating and implementing a gender-fair policy. Programme evaluation has revealed that partners are enthusiastic about this strategy, which offers them more long-term forms of accompaniment by local GAD experts. In fact, they have said that it makes Novib's insistence on their integrating a gender-based perspective acceptable. In 1991, Novib organised a workshop in Managua for gender experts on the possibilities and limitations of the role of the outside consultant.

The second group are locally based general consultants or experts in specific areas of development. Novib expects these consultants to approach evaluation, monitoring, and accompaniment from a development perspective into which gender is integrated. A recommendation from the Managua workshop mentioned above is that comparable workshops should be held for this kind of consultant. General workshops in the Netherlands with local consultants have been held recently.

Thematic working groups of partners

These groups offer a valuable opportunity for partners, frequently together with local consultants, to discuss their successes and failures in mainstreaming gender-fair policies. There are now nine working groups on gender: four in Latin America, four in Asia, and one in Africa. These are mixed groups containing experts from women's organisations and mixed NGDOs, and combining experience-sharing and policy debate between NGDOs. It is therefore important that both gender experts and directors or other senior NGDO personnel are represented on the working groups.

North/South linking projects

These are informational, educational, and lobbying projects which focus on making links and comparisons between Northern and Southern aspects of particular issues. One examples is a South/North Project on Sustainable Agriculture, in which research was done in the Netherlands and in Asia into alternative agricultural production practices and their constraints. Another example is a linking project with women's organisations in Latin America which resulted in the *Entre Mujeres* network, whose members are Northern and Southern, mixed and women's organisations. This is a lobbying network aiming to influence the policies of Southern NGDOs, donor organisations, and international bodies such as the World Bank, the EC, and UN institutions.

Support to Southern NGO networks

Novib is encouraging and financing NGO networks in the South to do work on issues relevant to Novib partners, with a focus on regional and international lobbying. A major example is Novib's international networking project on human rights and women's rights (see Case Study 9c).

All this work with reference to Southern partners must of course be underpinned by an internal policy of positive action towards women coherent with Novib's gender policy towards project partners. This is vitally important for Novib's credibility with partners. Novib's *Contours for Novib's policy concerning women: work-plan 1991–1993*, produced in April 1991, has set out a timetabled programme of actions for making Novib's policy on women a reality, both internally and externally.

Incorporating gender into Lomé IV projects and programmes

Dorothée Versteylen, Women's Officer, DG VIII, European Commission

Formulating a gender-fair policy

The European Community's policy on women in development, as formulated in various conclusions of the Council, aims to integrate women as agents and full beneficiaries into the mainstream of development. It focuses on improving women's income-earning capability and broader opportunities.

The basic principles of the policy are increasingly endorsed by non-industrialised countries of the South, as witnessed by the cooperation agreements between the EC and the Asian and Latin American countries, as well as by the Lomé Convention itself, which defines the framework for Community cooperation with 69 countries in Africa, the Caribbean, and the Pacific (ACP). In the third Lomé Convention (valid for the period 1985-1990) the issue of Women in Development was confined to one article in the Chapter dealing with socio-cultural cooperation; in the fourth Convention the WID theme is no longer isolated as a socio-cultural issue, but is integrated throughout the texts as an issue which is important for the economy and society as a whole.

The objectives of the Convention explicitly state that men and women must be able to participate and benefit on equal terms from ACP/EC development cooperation. This principle is then elaborated in the following chapters, especially those dealing with the sectors of agriculture, animal husbandry, and fisheries. Not only are the target populations, such as farmers, differentiated by gender, but the Convention recognises that for women to participate on equal terms with men, special measures are required in the framework of the various development projects and programmes. In addition, where EC support for structural adjustment programmes is discussed, women are being given attention as a specially vulnerable group.

Apart from this integration of the women's dimension in the chapters dealing with economic and technical cooperation, the special article devoted to the position of women which existed already in Lomé III has been maintained and further elaborated, in that it discusses — besides the need to improve the economic status of women — issues such as access to education, health care, family planning, and labour-saving technology.

So as far as the formulation of policy is concerned, much progress has been made. Formulating policy, however, is one thing; what counts is its *implementation*.

Implementing the policy

If women are to be integrated into the mainstream of development cooperation, a number of measures are required, both within the administrative systems of the donor — the European Commission, in this case — and at the political, administrative, and project levels in the recipient countries. In this context, I shall concentrate on the ACP countries.

At project level

To start at the level of projects, we see that the integration of women requires first of all research into the different tasks, responsibilities, needs, and opportunities of both men and women. The next step is that project design and appraisal has to be based on this gender-analysis, and measures have to be planned in terms of project staff, activities, and inputs, in order to make sure that men and women will benefit equally from the intervention. It is thus often the case that female staff need to be recruited, to work with the women from the target population. The agricultural extension and credit systems often need to be adapted in order to be made accessible to women. To enhance the participation of women, special activities should be undertaken, such as the training of project staff, literacy and technical training for women in the target population, and the introduction of labour-saving technology.

Such measures do, however, require financing — which is not necessarily a problem in the context of bilateral cooperation, in particular where 'Women in Development' figures among the priorities of the donor country. But in the framework of the Lomé Convention, finance can indeed be a problem. The reason is that the Convention limits the EC's potential for implementing policy — on whatever issue — and these limitations become particularly acute when it comes to policy concerning a still-sensitive issue like Women in Development.

ACP countries

The Lomé Convention is in law an agreement between two equal partners (the EC on the one hand and the ACP countries on the other). An important basic principle of the Convention is the right of the ACP countries to determine their own development models and strategies. Their cooperation with the EC will then serve to support their efforts.

Where the position of women is concerned, the Convention explicitly states that 'cooperation shall support the ACP-states' efforts aimed at enhancing the status of women ...'. In other words, if an ACP country does not undertake any effort, there will be little to support.

What does this mean in practice? To give one example: a couple of years ago, the Commission received a request for financial support for an extension of the Ahfad College in Sudan. This is a private university for women, with a good reputation, training women for positions in the private sector and in the government administration. With the government then in office, an agreement was reached to finance a consultancy study into the physical requirements (buildings and teaching materials) and the relevance of course contents. A financing proposal was duly made. In the meantime, however, the political situation in Sudan had changed radically, with the present government not altogether committed to promoting women's status; as a result, the Ahfad proposal was put aside.

We see, therefore, that the political context in a given country determines, to a great extent, what can be achieved. This is particularly true in the framework of the Lomé Convention, which operates on the principle that the authority to make decisions on the expenditure of the European Development Fund (EDF) rests largely with the recipient country. At the start of a Convention period, the EDF is divided according to certain criteria among the individual ACP countries, who then themselves decide — in consultation with the Commission and in accordance with the Convention — on the priorities for using the available funds.

This means that the EC cannot decide on its own to add female expertise to project staff, for example, or to commission a study of women's needs in a certain area, or to finance an interesting initiative from a local women's organisation — since this normally requires dipping into the EDF, which in principle is controlled by the ACP country concerned.

So funding measures to promote the participation of women is not straightforward for the EC, even though the participation of women is an objective of the Convention. The problems which arise, even in less extreme political situations than in Sudan, may be illustrated by a small incident which occurred half-way through the negotiations for Lomé IV, during a meeting of the EC/ACP Council of Ministers in Brazzaville. An official document, reflecting the recipient nations' point of view, stated that indeed women's roles and interests should be taken into account — 'as long as this would not slow down the project formulation'. It is true that this 'slip of the tongue' was quickly corrected, but it does indicate that the practical implementation of the WID policy will require negotiations in respect of each project, and that the initiative for such a discussion will usually lie with the Commission.

The European Commission

And here I come to the third level of development administration which is important for implementing WID policy: that of the Commission's own services. How and to what extent can the Commission ensure the integration of women in EC-financed development operations?

As in most donor administrations, it is the so-called WID Desk which is the moving force behind the formulation and implementation of WID policy. This desk was created in 1982 within the Directorate General for Development (DG VIII), which is responsible for cooperation with the ACP countries, while in 1990 a similar desk was installed in the Directorate General for External Relations (DG I), which is responsible for development cooperation with the Asian, Latin American, and Mediterranean countries.

The staffing of the desks — one person on each — is very limited, and has so far made it impossible for the desks to scrutinise individual funding proposals. Ideally, the WID desks should have sufficient resources to contribute to all stages of project preparation.

WID strategy

In this administrative context, the WID desk in DG VIII has adopted a pragmatic strategy, taking the line that every official in the department is responsible for the implementation of the Lomé Convention, and thus for the WID policy. It was important to ensure that staff with operational responsibility — that is, the country desks and the technicians in Brussels, as well as the staff in the Commission delegations in the ACP countries — should understand the issues of women in development, and receive training in gender-fair practice.

In other words, the WID desk concentrates on sensitisation programmes for staff, providing information and training, as well as making tools and expertise available. The desk has regularly organised training sessions with staff in Brussels, and also with Commission delegates on their visits to headquarters. The desk also initiated a task force which produces irregular issues of a WID Newsletter for colleagues in Brussels and overseas.

The WID desk's evaluation of a number of rural development projects in Malawi stimulated useful discussion and increased comprehension of women's issues, particularly on the part of management. The EC was funding several rural projects in Malawi which were very similar in design, except that one project had adopted a strategy for the participation of women, but the others had not. The mission report clearly demonstrated women's great interest in receiving agricultural inputs and advice, while at the same time it showed the potential of mainstream development projects to address these needs, on condition that appropriate measures are taken.

Acting on this mission report, it was decided to carry out a larger-scale evaluation of EDF projects implemented in four different sectors of rural development in eight African countries. This exercise produced a number of useful recommendations, which (supplemented by lessons learned from other agencies' guidelines) formed the basis of a Manual which I drew up in close collaboration with EC colleagues.

The Manual includes instructions and guidelines for incorporating women's concerns into the various phases of the project cycle, together with specific guidelines for the sectors of agriculture, animal husbandry, forestry, and drinking-water supply. In the near future we hope to add a section on the fisheries sector.

The introduction of this Manual is being followed by staff-training programmes in Brussels, and regional training workshops in Africa. The latter target staff in the Commission delegations, as well as high-level officials from ACP countries, who within the Ministries of Finance, Agriculture, and other technical ministries are involved in making decisions on EDF projects. In October 1992 we organised regional training for the first time for some 40 participants — more than half of whom were men — from eight African countries.

This first experience has been very positive. The participants are increasingly interested and motivated to apply a gender-fair approach to project-cycle management. This type of training, we are convinced, is a potentially important strategy for the implementation of WID policy.

We have also provided short-term technical assistance to the Commission delegations: a number of expert consultants have screened EDF programmes in several ACP countries — 20 so far — to identify projects which are in principle relevant to women. In collaboration with EC staff and the national authorities, they make operational recommendations for each WID-relevant project, for the strengthening of women's participation.

Results

Altogether, these activities have achieved a marked change in staff mentality. Where, a couple of years ago, the issue of Women in Development gave rise to jokes (if not undisguised aversion), and the conviction that such concerns were the hobby of Western feminists, the theme is now accepted as being one of the issues that need to be attended to, even if there is no common agreement yet on the 'how and when'. In general, there is a willingness to accept good operational advice, and to present this to the respective government authorities. Increasing attention is being paid to the roles and needs of women in the framework of feasibility studies or mid-term reviews, and in some cases this has led to the adaptation of project staffing, activities, and inputs.

This is the case in an irrigation project in Senegal, where female community-development workers have been appointed to organise women to claim better access to irrigated fields, agricultural extension, credit, and other project services.

In the framework of an agricultural project in Benin, the staffing of the project and the scope of the agricultural extension services have been adapted in order to respond to the needs of women farmers.

After a WID evaluation of a rural development programme in Togo, it has been decided to recruit a number of female field workers, to act as intermediaries in an Islamic context between rural women and male technical staff.

In an irrigation project in Burkina Faso which aims to improve swamp rice production, the majority of the participants are women. This is also the case in a sheep and goat development project in Botswana.

Women constitute a large part of the target population for several rural development projects in Nigeria. They do actively take part in activities like adult education, literacy training, primary health care, and family planning, and in a support programme for small-scale enterprises. In this latter field, a special effort is made to avoid conventional income-generating projects for women, and to select real profit-making enterprises. Various women's cooperatives have benefited from credit for agricultural machinery for the cultivation of rice, or other crops, on a relatively large scale. Women are trained in the handling and maintenance of machines, and in the elementary principles of book-keeping and management. The new enterprises and cooperatives are regularly visited by business management advisers.

In a forestry project, also in Nigeria, more than 4,000 women participate in the establishment of tree nurseries and the planting of trees. In the second phase of the project, women's groups will be trained and credit will be made available for animal-husbandry and agricultural investments.

Many projects in the fisheries sector, and in particular in artisanal fisheries and aquaculture, have built-in activities aimed at decreasing women's workload in the processing and marketing of fish through the introduction of improved technology, credit facilities, etc.

Apart from these cases where attention to women's roles and needs is an integrated part of mainstream development operations, specific actions for women are also undertaken. In some cases these are projects carried out with the Ministry of Women's Affairs, financed from the EDF, but more often they are co-financed NGO projects. It is interesting to note that the NGOs are slowly moving away from the conventional women's projects dealing with cooking, sewing, and handcrafts to more innovative schemes aimed at improving the status of women. Indeed, the NGO co-financing scheme can constitute an interesting channel, complementary to the official aid schemes, through which issues can be addressed like the legal status of women, sexual violence, female circumcision/infibulation, awareness-raising, and networking.

Conclusion and recommendations

Thus we see that in a variety of countries with quite different socio-cultural contexts, actions are possible to help women participate in and benefit from mainstream development operations in various sectors of the economy. But we are only at the beginning of the process, and unfortunately there are still too many projects which bypass women.

Certainly much progress has been made in the last couple of years. To a large extent, this has been possible thanks to a small budget line made available in 1991 by the European Parliament, which enabled the WID desk to hire external expertise. Money alone, however, is not enough: there needs to be sufficient staff in Brussels to implement, coordinate, and monitor the action programme.

The EC's delegations, usually staffed by an economist, one or two agronomists, and a civil engineer, need to be strengthened by the inclusion of staff trained in the area of gender and development. EC member states might help in this respect, by seconding academics who have studied gender and development to work with the delegations for limited periods.

A third area where the member states could play an important role concerns the need for capacity-building. While gender studies do exist in some member states, there is a need for expansion, particularly in the provision of fellowships to students from the South. Also the creation of gender-training courses at universities in the South, and the incorporation of gender issues in other development-related courses, is essential for the creation of expertise which will eventually benefit every phase of the project cycle. A more widespread academic capacity on gender and development within the member states of the European Community will contribute to better formulation and implementation of policy in their own bilateral work — which in turn will contribute to improved policy implementation in relation to women's needs at the Community level.

(Note: The contents of this paper are the sole responsibility of the author, and do not necessarily reflect the views of the Commission.)

Monitoring criteria: the experience of Novib

Ellen Sprenger

This paper will address a series of questions:

- How is monitoring organised within Novib's project department, and what is the place of gender monitoring within it?
- What are we monitoring? — Novib's project policy with partners and the instruments for implementing it.
- How is this monitoring implemented in-house and at partner level, and what is the interaction between these two arenas?

The context for monitoring: introduction to Novib

The Dutch NGDO Novib was founded in 1956. Its mandate included direct assistance to the poor; fundraising in order to generate the resources to do so; informing and educating the Dutch public; and exerting political pressure through advocacy. Its founding group included people from various walks of life: rebellious priests, academics, and civil servants with links to the foreign ministry. In countries in the South, Novib worked closely with staff of Dutch embassies.

Generating sufficient financial resources was a problem in those early days, and the Department of Foreign Affairs assisted frequently. This cooperation was institutionalised in 1965 in the first co-financing agreement between the Ministry of Foreign

Affairs and Novib. Soon three other co-financing agencies followed, including HIVOS in 1978. This first co-financing agreement was based on the awareness that NGOs play an important role in poverty alleviation. In the early days this role was predominantly seen as complementary to the more technocratic and macro-economic approach of the Ministry itself. In recent years NGOs are also increasingly being valued for their activities in the field of political advocacy.

In the 1970s, Novib acquired the reputation of being a socialist-leaning organisation. It made many links with like-minded organisations in the North, and its threefold strategy of project work with partners, development education work, and political lobbying has been maintained up to the present.

From the late 1970s onwards, Novib has become increasingly professionalised, employing academics and field-experienced staff, among other experts, and placing more emphasis on accountability, the production of annual reports, and other mechanisms.

Novib's growth over the past 15 years can be gauged from the following table:

	1977	1992
Total staff	71	255
Project Department staff	20	105
No. of projects	266	899
Turnover (Dfl.)	30.2m	160m (*c.* US$80m)

In 1992, Novib had 800 partner organisations in 45 different countries.

Monitoring: meeting two core objectives

We carry out monitoring in Novib in order to meet two central objectives. First, to show what we are doing and how Novib makes a difference, and to meet our responsibility of accountability to our constituency and the Dutch public in general, and to the Dutch Ministry of Foreign Affairs. The underlying objective here is to emphasise the importance of development cooperation in general and Novib's work in particular, and to promote a constantly growing interest in and knowledge of development issues and North/East/South relations among the Dutch public. A further objective here is to safeguard our sources of income and canvass others, in terms of co-financing (75 per cent of Novib's financial base in 1992) and fundraising (25 per cent in 1992).

The second objective of our monitoring is to contribute to a process of learning within Novib and among Novib's partners. This has the further objective of facilitating a process of continuous reflection aimed at operationalising Novib's mission statement, i.e. the alleviation of structural poverty and the achievement of sustainable development.

Monitoring, past and present

Monitoring is an activity aimed at understanding what you are doing: a process of reflection, of following progress made, and of planning ahead in the light of what is learned. It is a process that is continually taking place (but not always consciously, or deliberately) in every individual and every organisation. However, it is most valuable when it is done in a centralised and systematic way, bringing together a variety of experiences and following up on the new insights gained from the process.

Over the last few years, much work has been done on the systematisation of monitoring activities within Novib, and our computerised central monitoring system, applying both to Novib in general and to each department, has only recently become operational. The development of the central computerised monitoring system received a strong impetus from the elaboration in 1990 of an impact study and its recommendations.

The initiative for this study, which involved in-depth studies by independent researchers of a number of partner organisations, came from the four co-financing agencies in a joint attempt to contribute to the general debate on the quality of development cooperation. A strong point that came out of this study was the need for *improvement of the monitoring and evaluation system* in both co-financing agencies and partner organisations.

In the field of gender and development, the developing of monitoring initiatives and the quest for a central monitoring system had been under way since the mid-1980s (see below). These were considered important instruments for conscientisation on gender-linked issues and hence for the implementation of gender policies. Among the activities carried out were women's criteria checklists, research on strategies of women's projects, and an inventory of women's projects. However, the fact that there was no central system from which to extract information meant that these activities were very time-consuming. This revealed very clearly the strategic importance of a monitoring system that is disaggregated by gender. It was also learned that, apart from such a monitoring system, a positive attitude among staff members is needed. This pointed to the more general need to develop a so-called monitoring 'climate' within the organisation.

The projects department: building bricks of our policy

Novib's mission statement declares that:

> Novib's core objective is to contribute to sustainable development by means of structural alleviation of poverty and injustice, especially for marginalised groups in the South. In order to reach this goal of sustainability, Novib focuses specifically on the relationship between poverty and:
>
> * access to and control over natural resources;
> * gender-relations;
> * human rights.
>
> We do this by strengthening autonomous partner organisations and through the promotion and facilitation of networking and alliance-building with other organisations.

In its work Novib has opted for three priority themes, or rather lines of action: the environment, women, and human rights. A further important characteristic is that over the years a shift in policy has taken place, from a focus on the target-group level and project support towards a focus on partner organisations. In addition to this there is a focus on regional and national specificity. This policy is built basically on two convictions: first, the belief that projects and programmes need competent, strong organisations to ensure better and more sustainable performance

— hence the need for organisational strengthening; and second, the belief that strong NGOs and NGO networks play a key political role in strengthening civil society by facilitating processes of democratisation — hence the need for institutional development.

Within the projects department, important policy instruments are:

- platform meetings; seminars (issue-based and occasional); working groups on a more continuous basis; consultancies, particularly on priority areas; project monitoring and evaluation systems (PMEs); financial reporting; discussions on regional or country-specific issues (e.g. income generation, AIDS, etc.);
- conferences with consultants and partners in order to promote dialogue;
- national, regional, and international lobbying activities; promotion of strategic alliances; networking;
- building and strengthening structures for consultancy in the countries where we are active.

Monitoring instruments for project (partner) policy

Novib currently has an array of instruments for monitoring the implementation of policy at project or partner levels. These operate within the institution and as part of our on-going dialogue with partner organisations. These are some of the instruments:

Internal
- Multi-year planning, yearly planning, and quarterly reporting on progress made.
- A central, computerised monitoring system.
- Project and partner evaluations, at the end of a (usually) three-year time-frame of financial support. Also a yearly progress report from partners.

External
- Country and regional policy documents: these are drawn up and monitored during partner platform meetings.

- Partner profiles: in the process of implementation. The main objectives of a partner profile are: to facilitate the monitoring of stronger and weaker points and the effectiveness of partners; to strengthen the partners through dialogue with Novib and among partners; to strengthen the quality of the decision-making process concerning possible support of partners on a multi-annual perspective; as an instrument to increase the transparency of Novib's view of partners.

Monitoring gender and development: a brief history

Pressure to establish a more systematic approach and policy on what was then called WAD (women and development) dates back to the early 1980s. There was a strong internal lobby for it, but also pressure from partner organisations, particularly in Latin America. The change in the international climate as a result of the UN Decade for Women (1976-85) also played an important role. This was the period that saw the birth of Taskforce Women, at that point very much an advocacy group aiming for the institutionalisation of gender-fair practice, and the first policy document on gender and development was written (1983).

In the mid-1980s important steps were taken, with the establishment of a WAD officer in the projects department in 1986, a second general policy document, and research on women's projects. This study revealed that there was not enough information on the impact of programmes and projects on women in the target groups. Information about the position of women in partner organisations was also found to be lacking. Moreover, there were not enough women-specific projects. This too pointed to the need for developing a central and standardised monitoring system.

In the late 1980s, the WAD officer introduced a women's check-list, but did not succeed in getting it implemented. This was a list of issues raised by the involvement of women in projects, intended to facilitate discussion during the phase of project identification and approval. Although project officers generally agreed that the check-list was a useful instrument, it never really took root, because the checklist was extensive and the general monitoring activities of the department were not yet well enough developed to be able to use it adequately. In the end the list was reduced to four key issues to be considered when approving a project proposal:

• What are the main obstacles for women indicated in the analysis provided by the counterpart?

• Is there a separate women's section within an integrated project/programme? If not, chances are that the participation of women and the promotion of women's interests will be limited.

• Are the activities and the means of the project/programme as accessible to women as to men? If not, emphasise greater access and/or other means.

• What are the expected effects of the project/programme on women? Think of: division of labour; workload; access to production factors and information. If the position of women is made worse, turn down the project in the form presented.

Monitoring gender and development in-house

Since 1990 active in-house monitoring has been established. It was felt that visible targets were needed, rather than another policy document; thus for the 1990-93 period a practice-oriented three-year work-plan, aimed at implementation, was developed. The result was the formulation of *Contours for Novib's policy concerning women: work-plan 1991-1993*. The document has been adopted by Novib's board of directors, with whom, together with the heads of regional desks, ultimate responsibility for implementation rests in the final instance.

In the work-plan, a number of targets are formulated. These are the targets for the projects department:

• Terms of reference for projects will include gender-relevant issues.
• Missions (identification, scouting, monitoring, and evaluation) should include gender-sensitive people and at least one woman with gender expertise.
• Evaluation and project-approval memoranda should answer four main questions (these are the four questions summarising the previous women's checklist).
• Affirmative action should be taken in order to engage new female consultants.
• Novib should strive to increase the number of women's organisations as partners, aiming for a target of 10 per cent of all partners by the end of 1992.

At present (May 1993), it can be said that the first four of these targets are on-going and will be included in Novib's general monitoring criteria and procedures. In addition to this, the target of 10 per cent autonomous women's organisations has been met: in 1992 Novib supported 85 autonomous women's organisations (11 per cent).

Contours turned out to be an influential document, because of its practical orientation. In addition, it made the issue of gender clearly visible within the organisation and among partner organisations.

Monitoring gender and development at partner level

In Novib's relationship with its partners, monitoring is perceived as an essential element in a learning process whereby Novib acts as a facilitator, either directly, by participating in monitoring activities, or indirectly, by providing financial support for the recruitment of local consultants.

We have found that partner organisations increasingly express a need for guidance or other forms of support to strengthen them in their gender policy and implementation. Novib asks partner organisations to reflect and report on progress made in this field, and in that sense they are under a certain pressure to answer to these questions. At the same time, processes of change are also taking place among target groups, among individual NGO staff members, and in the national climate. NGO platforms, which provide a forum for discussion and consultation for NGOs in a country (not necessarily all Novib partners) and in which women's organisations have a high profile, are now being set up in a number of countries, and are also a catalyst in encouraging partners to seek guidance and advice on their gender policy.

A variety of responses from partners is encountered, forming successive stages in a learning process:

• Avoidance/defence mechanisms are aroused. This occurs in a very few cases.

• Women are put on the agenda and some women-specific activities are initiated. The focus here tends to be on short-term, immediate needs (*first-step learning*). (There is a danger, however, that at this stage gender issues are being paid lip-service only, for reasons of ensuring continued funding.)

• Women are on the agenda, but, more importantly, the shift has been made towards identifying gender-relations, as the source of imbalances of power between men and women, as the core issue to address. The organisations are in the process of making internal changes, such as introducing affirmative action or making the connection between short-term immediate needs and long-term strategic interests. They are often in need of support and backing, such as help from consultants (*second-step learning*).

We have developed one successful format that contributes to the development of a gender-based perspective and policy: *gender working groups*, in which representatives of partner organisations participate. The objective of these partner groups is to strengthen mixed organisations in particular. Representatives of women's organisations and other gender experts act as facilitators in the working groups. The idea is to promote exchange among partners and cross-fertilisation between gender agents and others, and thus generate a multiplier effect. In some cases lobby activities were taken up collectively. The workshops focus on three levels: internal policy development; analysis and planning; project implementation and relationships with target groups. Currently, nine working groups are active on a more or less continuous basis (in Indonesia, Thailand, the Philippines, India, Mexico, Peru, Colombia, Southern Africa, and Burkina Faso).

Working groups and workshops of this kind also take place on other issues: the environment, project monitoring and evaluation (PMEs), and financial reporting. They not only contribute to organisational strengthening and institutional development, but are also a forum where partners can discuss policy issues that result in regional and country-specific policy documents.

Three monitoring instruments

Below we describe briefly three of the instruments which Novib has developed for monitoring, both in-house and overseas.

Classification forms

This monitoring instrument is used in-house only. It is filled in after formal approval of a project, and the objective is to be able to classify partners into specific categories. With regard to gender, these are:

- autonomous women's organisation (both intermediary and target group);
- partner organisation with a gender component (those described earlier as having arrived at first-step learning);
- partner organisation with an integrated gender-based perspective (those that have arrived at second-step learning).

At project level, a distinction is made between women's projects and projects with an integrated gender-based perspective.

Country/regional policy documents

These focus on planned gender-related activities which have been discussed and agreed upon during a partner platform meeting. The objective is to have such platform meetings in all countries where Novib is active, in order to develop a multi-annual policy in dialogue with partners. In a number of areas these platform meetings take place in each (sub)region.

Issues related to gender planning may include building and/or strengthening consultancy networks by increasing the number of women in them or emphasising the need for gender-sensitive participants; setting up working groups on gender and planning activities around them; running other seminars; identifying new partners active in the field of GAD.

Partner profiles

An important function of a partner profile is to systematise the information necessary for organisational and institutional support and the strengthening of partner organisations. Focal points from a GAD perspective are:

Institutional development
- Strategic alliances or other linkages with autonomous women's organisations and/or women's networks.
- Participation in lobbying activities on gender-related issues.

Organisational development
- Affirmative action for women.
- Special facilities for women, such as (access to) training for women's officers and women staff; maternity and childcare facilities; flexible labour conditions such as part-time and/or job-sharing arrangements.
- Presence of GAD expertise, either in-house or via consultants,

at various levels in the organisation. Structures for ensuring gender-fair practice within the organisation should be systematically utilised, planned, and budgeted for.
- Activities contributing to the general gender-sensitisation of staff (staff development).

Programme level
- Analysis of gender-relations among target group.
- Active participation of women in programme design and implementation.
- Women's access to and control over programme benefits.
- Consideration of arguments to opt for either a gender-specific or a gender-integrated approach.
- Monitoring and evaluation of impact of gender policies on the target group.

Ibis' partner organisations

Diana Vinding

Who are Ibis' partners?

The Danish NGDO Ibis works with approximately 70 partner organisations overseas. These embrace a wide variety of bodies: government ministries (four in Namibia, two in Nicaragua); municipalities (one in Namibia, two in Nicaragua); popular organisations, such as peasants' organisations, trade unions (approximately 20 in all, covering all countries where Ibis cooperates, except Chile); NGOs (40, covering all countries).

Among these partners are women's organisations. Ibis works with three independent women's organisations, all in South Africa, and several women's sections affiliated to peasants' organisations and trade unions in a number of countries. Women's organisations are also among Ibis-supported small-scale projects (defined as those with a maximum funding level of US$45,000).

A breakdown of Ibis' partners in terms of their attitude to gender reveals the following pattern: two (both in Chile) are feminist-oriented; two or three are gender-aware; 19 are fairly gender-aware; 46 are not gender-aware.

Ibis' criteria for choosing partners

In choosing partners, Ibis operates on the principle that collaboration should be built on the partner's own strategy and objectives. This principle has entailed the establishment of a number of important criteria. In the organisation's first phase, political likemindedness was important, considered necessary from the point of view of active solidarity. Nowadays the most important requirement is that partners should have a participative approach, integrating target groups into every stage of project design, planning, and implementation. To a lesser extent (because these are supposedly included in these more general criteria) Ibis looks for positive attitudes and good practice in certain concrete areas, namely: human rights, the environment, and women. In this last aspect, Ibis now looks for partners with a positive attitude towards gender-fair development.

Critical issues

Conditionality or not?

DANIDA has a policy of conditionality as regards human rights when proposing programmes and partners to the Danish government, making reference to the UN Convention on Women (CEDAW). DANIDA's thinking is that gender should be given the same importance as respect for human rights in this regard.

Ibis, on the other hand, operates no policy of conditionality, for the reasons indicated above: Ibis seeks partnership on equal terms and with a strong emphasis on the participative approach and processes of dialogue.

Attitudes of partners

Given that the majority of Ibis' present partners cannot be classified as gender-aware, partners' attitudes to gender-fair development often constitute a constraint. A variety of attitudes and tactics of indifference and resistance is encountered, including a total lack of interest or understanding; paying lip-service to gender in project applications and neglecting or boycotting it at the point of implementation; manipulation of personnel in charge of the women's aspect of a programme or project, either by paying a lower salary or even by making open or covert threats of dismissal; labelling as 'feminist' (with a pejorative connotation) everything that challenges male domination/influence (usually invoking fears of jealousy and infidelity, liable to lead to divorce and family breakdown).

Recommended strategy

What strategy can be used to counter these forms of resistance? Ibis has found that the most effective strategy is to establish dialogue with partners, and to offer institutional support in the form of training or consultancy on gender issues.

It can also be helpful to use concepts of human rights as a lever to make the partner organisation admit the legitimacy of women's strategic needs and to see them as true rights: the right to work, the right to leisure, the right to personal freedom (such as a woman's right to decide for herself whether to go to a meeting), the right to control her own body and decide the number of children she will have, and the right to a life free from violence.

Another strategy is to develop a trust-building approach, for instance through encouraging non-threatening activities for women, in order to dispel myths about the dangers to family life if women become active outside the home.

Although Ibis has sometimes found it counter-productive to work with a directly feminist approach, feminist organisations can be important as critical, innovative sources of ideas and inspiration, and a future strategy will be to consult them when overall policies and similar issues are being discussed.

Networking to improve our practice: Oxfam's South/South Women's Linking Project

Candida March

This account concentrates on the experiences gained from the Women's Linking Project, a three-year project coordinated by the Gender and Development Unit of Oxfam (UK and Ireland). It will attempt to give a glimpse of the methodology of the project itself, its rationale, and some of the lessons we have learned from it.

Rationale

Very broadly, this project tries to respond to the need for greater understanding and communication of gender as a development issue; for a closer dialogue between South and North; for alternative strategies for gender-fair development and North/South cooperation; and for gender-fair policies and programmes in Northern funding agencies, ones that incorporate Southern women's perspectives.

More specifically, the Women's Linking Project is consulting Southern women, in order to build gender-fair practice and policy that are sensitive to Southern women's experiences. It also tries to produce a basis on which to lobby Southern and Northern NGOs for change in their gender policies.

Oxfam works through a large number of field offices, some of which are fairly distant from the women's movement, while others are leading with examples of best or near-best practice.

This project is using networking to promote and explore examples of best practice and to increase Oxfam's contact with Southern organisations working on gender-fair issues. The project also sets out to create solidarity and information-sharing exchanges and informal networks for Southern NGOs, Oxfam staff, and like-minded NGOs, in order for them to learn cross-regionally and break through the isolation that many feel.

Finally, through communication and exchanges, the project is promoting gender as a development issue to the British and Irish public.

Stages of the project

The project is being implemented by a core group and advisory group of Southern women and Oxfam and through our field offices, promoting closer work with partners.

The South/North visit, March 1992

Eight women from Southern countries came to the UK and Ireland to communicate to the public, forge solidarity links, and build alliances around key issues: violence; health and reproductive rights; poverty and sustainable development; and culture. They met with a range of organisations and groups across Britain and Ireland.

The rationale behind the visit was to identify commonalties and differences as the basis for forging alliances; to promote Southern women's perspectives of aid and other macro-issues; to communicate to the public women's roles as agents for change.

Considerable spontaneous follow-up has taken place between the participating groups and the Southern women, including the development of joint initiatives and concrete solidarity actions. But follow-up would undoubtedly have been greater if we had had a more concrete strategy.

The consultation process

This is taking two forms: firstly, consultation by our field officers, in-country, to produce case studies and an internal review of our work; and secondly, regional meetings with women from Southern NGOs to identify their priority issues and strategies and the role that agencies like Oxfam can play.

International meetings

A major international meeting is planned for February 1994. The conclusions of the second stage of the project will be brought together on a global basis. Delegates from the regional meetings will come together to consolidate their findings. They will then attend an international conference with Oxfam staff, where they will meet to identify possible strategies around the theme of North/South cooperation and Oxfam's role.

Communication

Finally, we will do communication and follow-up work, including networking, advocacy, and preparation for the Beijing conference.

What are the lessons?

What are the lessons from this mainly face-to-face networking, and what is its potential impact on our gender work? What I am describing here is mainly WLP's direct experience, but it is similar to other initiatives undertaken by Oxfam, particularly in its fiftieth anniversary year.

First, this is a high-risk, high-reward process. It is a process fraught with contradictions and sometimes conflict; but at the same time it can be a very empowering process which allows and encourages alliance-building and information-sharing. It is a very powerful and energising way of learning, expanding analysis, picking up new ideas.

Successes

The North/South visit provided an excellent platform for Southern women to speak, and good opportunities for dialogue and a better understanding of each other's situation, North/South and South/South. It also succeeded in raising interest about Southern concerns in development in the British and Irish women's organisations and community base groups visited. And it helped to put gender-fair development more clearly on the map in Oxfam itself. Interestingly, it provided opportunities for Oxfam outreach workers and other organisations to strengthen, and in many cases initiate, contacts with community-based organisations and groups that had not seen working with Oxfam as a prime concern. The visits increased Oxfam's credibility with, and relevance to, community-based groups who, because of the WLP, began to see Oxfam as an agency with something to say on gender issues. This generated a lot of interest and sometimes surprise.

Unresolved issues

But at times this type of networking and consultation can be difficult. It is a process which brings to the forefront many unresolved issues for development agencies, such as:

• *The meaning and nature of partnership*, of cooperation, of control of decision-making processes. In particular, working with a core group of Southern NGOs has been problematic for Oxfam. This was a project whose primary aim was to influence Oxfam, which was funded by Oxfam, and which needed to adhere to very rigid Oxfam procedures. Yet the majority in the decision-making group were non-Oxfam people. Where should decision-making lie in a case like this? Where in reality does power lie?

In addition, different views of what the project should be trying to achieve, and South/North mistrust, continue to surface at times.

• *Representation*: whose voice? What legitimacy? For example, should we be consulting NGOs or the grassroots; feminists (concerned to develop new roles for women) or 'womanists' (concerned to make their traditional roles easier to fulfil)? It was made clear that there is no one Southern voice; but we should be wary of using this concept of 'no Southern voice' to deny Southern voices.

• *The complexity of the women's movement*: while women may have a common agenda, they often have very different ways of addressing the issues and different constraints placed on them.

• *The different identities involved*: there were times where tensions made things very difficult.

The most valuable lessons we learned

We learned the dangers of assuming a common agenda or underestimating the barriers to be overcome. Such barriers include cultural barriers, different styles of communication; differing priorities; hidden agendas, or suspicion of them; the whole history of relationships between the South and the North; and the use of power and influence.

At times these barriers can be higher than any common agendas such as feminism or North/South cooperation. A particularly high hurdle appears to be the South/North divide. In Oxfam we have learned the dangers of underestimating the degree of mistrust and antagonism that can exist towards Northern funding agencies. In trying to build South/North cooperation, both sides in the equation need to recognise their limitations and the different constituencies to whom they are accountable.

Another valuable lesson was the importance of time and space. If barriers are to be overcome, the process needs to allow plenty of time and lack of pressure for people to come to understand each other and for reflection. This has important implications for the number of concrete outputs that should be built into any such programme.

Conclusion

Feedback from the consultations we have undertaken so far has shown that Southern women's groups and local organisations are keen to be involved in these areas of Oxfam's work, and enthusiastic about networking and working with each other.

We believe that the project has taught us all much about the nature of partnership between North and South; about the need to provide a platform for Southern voices; and about the value of networking as a legitimate tool of development and a powerful tool for the marginalised.

WIDE: a European network for lobbying

Helen O'Connell, Chair, WIDE

Women in Development Europe (WIDE) is a European network of women and development national networks, non-governmental organisations, and individual women who are active on women and gender and development issues. It was founded in 1985 following the Nairobi Women's Conference. At present national platforms in around 14 countries are involved, mainly members of the European Community, but also non-EC countries; women from Austria, Switzerland are members, for example, and the network is building links with Eastern Europe.

WIDE receives funding from the European Commission, from non-governmental organisations, and from some governments. We have a small secretariat in Brussels with a new full-time coordinator, Mieke van der Veken. WIDE's Steering Group consists of one elected representative from each country, and it meets three times each year. We also have a small Bureau which meets more frequently. At present, WIDE has two main working groups: one on environment and population issues and the follow-up to the Rio conference; the other on WIDE's analysis of development and on preparations for the 1995 UN Women's Conference. We have an annual assembly where as many members as possible meet to exchange information, discuss issues, and decide on WIDE's priorities.

WIDE has four main aims:

• To exchange information and build up more expertise on

issues of importance to women's development needs in developing countries, with a view to deepening and extending public awareness of these issues.

• To encourage and strengthen the national networks, development policies, priorities, and programmes of European countries which are directed towards Southern countries, with a view to improving support for women in the South and Southern women living in the North.

• To promote purposeful contacts with women in partner countries, so that their development priorities will become the guiding principles of WIDE's activities.

• To lobby European and international institutions.

For WIDE, lobbying is an essential role. As a European network we are in a better position than Southern women's organisations to press for changes in the policy and programmes of those institutions which determine development choices for most Southern countries, such as the World Bank, the IMF, the European Community, and our bilateral development cooperation agencies. WIDE focuses primarily on the European Commission and European governments, with a view to informing and influencing their policies towards the South in general and towards Southern women in particular.

Lobbying work

Our lobbying work contains several key elements.

Clarifying our analysis

WIDE is committed to explicitly addressing issues of class and race, alongside gender issues. We are giving high priority to clarifying and deepening our analysis of European societies from a feminist and a gender-based perspective. We are seeking to redefine a development approach which includes the North.

Strengthening North/South alliances

A key part of WIDE's activities since 1985 has been building links with Southern women's networks, especially DAWN (Development Alternatives with Women for a New Era). We have taken every opportunity to talk with DAWN members, to invite them to our meetings, to participate in theirs. WIDE regards North/South alliances as extremely important in creating greater understanding and trust between North and South; in creating the potential for greater solidarity and for a strong international voice on the issues of women's rights.

In 1991/92, WIDE and DAWN worked together on environment issues and shared a platform at the Rio Conference. The process leading to the UN Women's Conference in 1995 is now providing WIDE, DAWN, ALT-WID (a US women's network), and others with a framework in which to work together. It has been agreed that WIDE, DAWN, and ALT-WID will share a platform at the 1995 conference, that we will work towards putting forward a shared view, including a critique of 'development' policy as we know it North and South, and perspectives on alternative development approaches.

Strengthening alliances in Europe

We are strengthening our alliances within Europe in order to break down the divisions that exist between women's organisations who work on international issues and those who work on national issues, like health care, equal opportunities, or violence. Thus we want to work much more closely with women's organisations and networks who focus on domestic or national issues. We are building strong links with organisations of Southern women who live in Europe, and now that we have moved our office to Brussels, we aim to establish close collaboration with other European networks, such as EUROSTEP, APRODEV, and EURODAD.

EC and European government policy

In addition to work on human rights, population issues, and the 1995 conference, WIDE will place particular emphasis in the coming years on European Community and European government relations with Southern countries. We will focus on both policy and practice. For example, we want to support and strengthen the progress already made within the Commission on women and development policy, monitoring and evaluation, and gender training of EC officials and delegations.

WIDE is a small network with limited resources, so we are very keen to work with others to strengthen our collective voices on gender and development issues.

Networking for human rights: Novib's experience

Mirjam van Reisen

First steps: the human rights conference

In April 1992 Novib organised the 'Marla Elena Moyano' conference in Holland on the inter-relationship between human rights, democracy, and development, named in commemoration of a Peruvian community women's organiser murdered by the Sendero Luminoso guerrillas. The conference was a first step in preparation for the World Conference on human rights in Vienna in 1993; and it also had the intention of improving the human rights policy of Novib itself.

There were difficulties in treating gender as a special issue in the conference, since the whole debate on human rights, democracy, and development was already very large and complicated. So, after discussion, we decided to integrate gender into the whole programme, rather than make it a special topic, but to ensure a 50:50 gender balance in both speakers and participants. Our regional bureaux were asked to send us a selection of people to be invited to the conference, and it was made very clear to them that delegates would be selected on the basis of a 50:50 division. We achieved this in terms of both participants and speakers.

At the conference itself, women raised spontaneous demands: first, for their own forum in the conference where they could address the issue of human rights, democracy, and development from the basis of gender; and, in parallel with this, to have women sitting in all the other discussion groups so that considerations of gender would be integrated into all the conference topics. The results were very positive: there were specific recommendations on human rights, and gender was included in the various topics of the conference. This meant that women and human rights featured explicitly in the conference report; and this had the further result that Novib management was encouraged to respond.

Integrating gender into the multi-annual plan

Between July and September 1992 Novib's multi-annual planning was discussed. Since there had been so much emphasis on women at the human rights conference, it was a good moment to include an integrated approach to women, human rights, and the environment in the multi-annual plan, which is in force up to 1996. This was approved later in 1992, for the project, education, and lobby departments.

Getting women on to the human rights agenda

In October 1992 I attended a meeting in New York to prepare for the 1993 World Conference on Human Rights to be held in Vienna. Based on the multi-annual plan, the mandate was formulated so as to include specifically a gender-based dimension within the general human-rights and development debate. The meeting in New York was not expected to focus on gender; but together with some other women in the meeting we were able to raise the question of gender as a possible main focal point of the preparatory meeting for the organisations who were present at the meeting, and get this agreed.

Forming a reference group

One point of concern was that in this group meeting for the preparations for the World Conference, there were no women's organisations or people who had worked on gender and human rights. I was worried that this would become an isolated exercise, especially as women's organisations in the United States were already working on a big campaign to include women's rights on the World Conference agenda and to focus on violations of women's human rights. So we formed a reference group, and invited on to it two key lobbyists on women and human rights, both partner organisations of Novib: the International Commission of Jurists, based in Geneva, and the International Human Rights Law Group, based in Washington/New York — both professional human rights organisations that include social and economic rights in their work. We further invited onto the network six regional networks working on women and development and also working within a human rights framework. In this way we were able to connect within our lobby:

- human rights networks, who could contribute professional human rights expertise on how to work on the World Conference;
- the women's organisations, who could specifically raise the women's agenda and experience from the women's lobby itself;
- the development organisations, who could bring in the development perspective, the Southern perspective, and could link the lobby to more general development organisations and to Southern women's groups.

The first meeting of this reference group was held in the Netherlands and organised by the Women's Council of the Dutch development organisations, which was focusing on preparations for the World Conference. This meeting produced a strategy for further work. The group would take on two activities. First, it would collect information from the networks, exchange information via fax, etc. Every network would take responsibility for faxing information on to national or local human rights, women's, and development organisations. This proved to be very useful, because the professional international human-rights organisations were working on issues about which the Southern groups knew nothing, and vice versa. There were many common strategies, but they were not in touch with each other.

The statement for the final PrepComm

The reference group's other task was to prepare a statement for the final PrepComm in Geneva in April 1993. We decided this would be the best time to lobby, because most issues would be discussed in Geneva and brought to Vienna only for approval by delegations. The International Human Rights Law Group was asked to prepare a statement, which they did in consultation with the women's coordinating networks in New York and the women's networks from the South in the reference group. Novib took on the job of preparing a list of organisations which could be asked to endorse the statement as soon as it was ready. The completed statement was faxed to all our EUROSTEP partner organisations and to all the participants at the previous year's Novib conference (including human rights organisations, development organisations, and women's organisations), and to international human rights organisations. This meant that a whole new network of organisations was now included in the women's agenda.

The response was very good. The international organisations sometimes took up to four days to discuss whether or not they should endorse the statement and whether or not to take a position on gender and human rights, which was an important process. From some of the Southern organisations we received very encouraging responses. One women's organisation wrote to us that with this initiative we had passed beyond the era of donor-recipient relations and had become real friends! About 90 organisations endorsed the statement, including many EUROSTEP members.

One result of the lobby was that after very long debates among the delegations, it had been decided that the conference would give special attention to 'vulnerable groups': women, children, indigenous people, workers, etc. The chair of the meeting, a woman, announced just before lunch that this point would be included in the draft, but under the wording 'special attention to women and children **and** vulnerable groups, such as indigenous people, workers, etc.', because it had already been agreed that women are not a vulnerable group.

What have we learned?

We have learned that it is very important to define your own position as an organisation very clearly, so as not to create tension, distrust, false competition. You have to define yourself as additional and as a facilitator, and that is not always easy.

There is tension between our engagement in lobbying and in funding. Sometimes it is hard to know whether organisations are working with you because you share the same vision of a lobby, or because there might be some other benefits from cooperation.

You must be flexible. If you are integrating gender, human rights, and development, you must be able to take on board other issues which might come up, which could be important; in this case it was the universality of human rights, which needed a very urgent response.

One thing we didn't succeed in doing was including women from Eastern European countries, and I think that is very important. Eastern Europe is a 'blind spot' and a region that we must begin to incorporate in our work.

Finally, this experience has led us to think about how to contribute to the Beijing conference and to the Social Summit, which will take place just before the Beijing conference, in Copenhagen, and which will probably divert a lot of attention away from the women's conference. How can we work from a specific gender-based perspective and also integrate our concerns into the mainstream? Should we focus on the Social Summit, or Beijing, or both? This is one of the questions we are debating at the moment.

Networking: the experience of the GOOD group in APRODEV

Gerlind Melsbach, Brot für die Welt

What is GOOD?

The GOOD working group is a group working on gender and development within the APRODEV network of European Protestant NGOs. GOOD stands for *Gender Orientation on Development*.

The GOOD working group and the GOOD process began in 1990. The initiative came mainly from the Dutch NGO ICCO. ICCO does not have a women's desk, but a desk which they call the 'emancipation desk', which is a name I like because it refers to the structures in our own society and worldwide. The first agencies to get involved were ICCO, together with member organisations of AG-KED — a rather complicated structure grouping our Protestant development agencies in Germany, to which Bread for the World and EZE also belong — and Christian Aid. A group consisting mainly of women engaged in gender work or WID work came together with the initial objective of exchanging information about what was going on with regard to gender in each individual agency. We also cooperate very closely in other areas, with many co-funded projects.

As a process slowly developed, objectives and goals changed. I will simply summarise them, without going into details about the process. One objective was gradually to enlarge the GOOD working group and include in the process the Scandinavian agencies, with whom our contact was more tenuous, and the Swiss agencies, mainly HEKS. We are still growing slowly.

Structure

Our structure is basically a core-group structure, with a core group consisting of one representative each from the four agencies from Holland, Christian Aid, Germany, and the Scandinavian agencies. We also cooperate very closely with the women's desk of the World Council of Churches and the Lutheran World Federation, which are both based in Geneva; but they are not directly members of the GOOD process.

Objectives and goals

Our main goals are to exchange information and learn from each other, with the purpose of strengthening the gender-linked work in our organisations; to work for change in our development cooperation so that it contributes more to empowering women in the South through our funding; and to learn from each other's policy and its implementation.

A wider objective, towards which we are moving only slowly, is that of questioning the current prevailing development paradigms and contributing a gender-based perspective to the development of new concepts. This is extremely difficult at this time, because so many concepts have broken down, and we are all feeling a lack of direction now, not only women.

Coordination and linking

Subsequently, we decided to make close links with APRODEV, although this was not an initial objective. This has the advantage that, if the EC level becomes more important, we can put our ideas forward through APRODEV, encouraging it to work more strongly and meaningfully from a gender perspective.

We coordinate with Southern networks, partners, and umbrellas, not necessarily all partner organisations, but also networks beyond our immediate partner networks; as well as coordinating and exchanging with other European networks like EUROSTEP, WIDE, and Euro-CIDSE.

The process as it has evolved so far

Our first idea was to have a North/South exchange. However, this was not possible immediately, because we first needed to become clearer among ourselves about our concepts and also to develop a common language. At the beginning there was a lot of misunderstanding, because terms were understood differently by different people, and experiences were different. As a result we replanned the GOOD process in a series of phases: first, a North/North process; second, a South/South process; and third, a North/South process. But this does not mean that in the North/North process only Northern agencies are represented: we have always consulted with Southern women, too,. and they have been present at our meetings whenever possible. At the moment we are somewhere between the North/North and the South/South phases.

Achievements so far

In terms of exchanging information and strengthening gender work in our own organisations, the experience has been very valuable. Our normal experience of doing work in our organisations is that you are isolated, you have no working partners, and you get somehow caught up in the mainstream. Networking has proved extremely useful, for instance, in terms of gender training. The Dutch and English agencies were much further advanced in training than we were in Germany: we had nobody who could conduct gender training, nor any idea how to develop a framework or a concept for gender training. So the process was hastened by these contacts through the gender working group.

In general, working with GOOD has had a very positive effect in advancing and strengthening our work in our own organisations. Sometimes we also find that individual desks in our organisations are cut off from important developments at the management level and from conceptual work; they are not so fully integrated organisationally. Networking helps us to get a clearer picture of these developments: sometimes you can get information from outside the organisation which you should get from within it!

The biggest step our whole process has taken up to now was a conference we organised last year in Germany, where the Scandinavian agencies participated for the first time. Resource people from Southern countries were present — from India, the Caribbean, and a representative from Femnet in Africa. Exchange was mainly on gender training as a tool; we exchanged lessons from our very short experience of working in this field in the North, and heard of the experiences and roles of the Southern women.

The outcome of the conference was very positive. It enhanced and intensified the GOOD process, and helped to institutionalise it. We now need greater capacity and also a coordinator at the European or APRODEV level. We are in the process of getting approval of a proposal for a coordination office, with a specific remit to facilitate the South/South process and organise a North/South conference in three years' time.

SECTION V

Appendices

What is EUROSTEP?

The 1990s pose a major challenge to European NGDOs. The end of the Cold War has resulted in the increased marginalisation of many parts of the South. Development policies, largely defined in the North, do not address the real needs of the majority of people in developing countries, many of whom are faced with deteriorating living conditions.

In a Europe which is moving towards economic and political integration, NGDOs are faced with the need to work together to influence policy decisions that affect people in developing countries. **European Solidarity Towards the Equal Participation of People (EUROSTEP)** has been established to fulfil this task.

European integration

In 1993 the Single Market has taken European integration a step forward, removing internal barriers on trade and commerce within the European Community. Discussions have already started on reforms leading to political integration in Europe, including the increased centralisation of policy decision-making, the establishment of a single external policy, and possibly in defence.

Influencing European policy

Policy decisions affecting developing countries are made at different levels. EUROSTEP enables its members to work on common strategies in their policy advocacy at national, European, and international levels. Working with other networks, it ensures that maximum pressure can be exerted on policy-makers in Europe.

EUROSTEP members are European NGDOs actively involved in Asia, Africa, and Latin America. EUROSTEP brings together 22 non-denominational NGDOs from 15 countries that share a similar approach to development. They combine their resources and capacity to influence development policies within Europe.

EUROSTEP has a small secretariat, based in Brussels, to facilitate its work and monitor the institutions of the European Community.

EUROSTEP's programme

Five themes have been chosen on which to focus joint action:

- Environment and development
- Debt
- European integration
- International trade and development
- African recovery and development.

The implementation of these programmes draws on experiences from local communities and seeks to bring these to discussions on development policy. The full participation of people in their own development, and in particular the role of women, is central to EUROSTEP's programmes. In addition to these main themes, EUROSTEP provides a framework for members to work together on policy issues relating to other topics, such as human rights and democracy, conflict, aid, immigrants, and geographical areas such as the Horn of Africa, the Middle East, and Central America.

EUROSTEP member organisations

ActionAid, UK
CNCD, Belgium
Concern, Ireland
Deutsche Welthungerhilfe, Germany
Frères des Hommes, France
Groupe Développement, France
Helinas, Greece
Hivos, Netherlands
Ibis, Denmark
Intermon, Spain
KePa, Finland
Mani Tese, Italy
Mellemfolkeligt Samvirke (MS), Denmark
Molisv, Italy
NCOS, Belgium
Norwegian People's Aid, Norway
Novib, Netherlands
Oikos, Portugal
Oxfam (UK and Ireland)
Save the Children Fund, Sweden
Swiss Aid Agencies Coalition
Terre des Hommes (BRD), Germany

Workshop programme

Enhancing our Experience: Gender Planning in EUROSTEP Agencies

A EUROSTEP Workshop
The Cherwell Centre, Oxford, UK
25–28 May 1993

Day 1: 26 May

Focus
Mainstreaming gender in our organisations

Objectives
- to discuss how different EUROSTEP agencies define mainstreaming gender at different levels;
- to provide an opportunity to share a critical assessment of how gender has been integrated into the programmes of EUROSTEP agencies;
- to identify common strategies and problems in order to make recommendations for strengthening agencies' work on gender.

Keynote speakers
- Georgina Ashworth, CHANGE: 'Institutionalising gender: an ABC'
- Naila Kabeer, Institute of Development Studies, Sussex University: 'Gender aware policy and planning: a social-relations perspective'

Working groups

1 The role of policy in mainstreaming gender
2 The role of staff development and gender training in mainstreaming gender
3 Defining the best structure to promote gender in our organisations: a separate desk or full integration into the work of all staff?
4 Working on gender issues with partner agencies and women's organisations in the South

Day 2: 27 May

Focus

Frameworks for programme and project planning

Objectives

* to look at the approaches and frameworks used by different agencies in integrating gender into programme and project planning;
* to discuss what works better in project appraisal, in our experience.

Keynote speakers (morning session)

* Dorothea Versteylen, Women's Desk, DG VIII, Commission of the European Community: 'The EC framework to assess gender issues in project appraisal'
* Tina Wallace, Planning and Evaluation Unit (Oxfam UK/Ireland): 'Integrating gender issues into evaluation'

Working groups (morning session)

5 Small group discussion on the following themes:
* What are our agencies' main long-term objectives in integrating gender?
* How do we put these objectives into practice in our regional and/or country programmes?
* What opportunities and constraints arise?

Keynote speakers (afternoon session)

* Sarah White, School of Development Studies, University of East Anglia: 'Making men an issue: do we need gender planning for the other half?'

- Judy El-Bushra, ACORD: 'Planning projects in situations of war: key considerations'

Working groups (afternoon session)

6 Consulting and involving local women in project design: strategies and difficulties
7 Integrating gender into project design: mixed and women-only projects
8 Monitoring criteria: how do we develop and implement them?

Day 3: 28 May

Focus
Networking for change

Objectives

- to share interesting and innovative experiences;
- to work towards identifying mechanisms to strengthen the gender work of EUROSTEP;
- to identify priority areas and strategies for lobby-oriented networking.

Panel presentation

- Networking to improve our practice: Oxfam/UK's South/South linking project
- WIDE (Women in Development Europe): a European network for lobbying
- Networking for human rights: the Novib experience
- The experience of the GOOD (Gender Orientation on Development) group in APRODEV

Working groups

9 Strengthening the gender network to improve development practice in EUROSTEP
10 Networking strategies for lobbying

Special working group

11 Planning a lobbying strategy in preparation for the 1994 Cairo World Conference on Population and Development

Closing session and recommendations

Workshop participants

ABANTU FOR DEVELOPMENT
Wanjiru Kihoro
41 Chessington House
Union Grove
London SW8 2RV
UK
Tel: 071 498 9324
Fax: 071 379 0801

ACORD
Judy el Bushra — Gender Officer
Francis House
Francis Street
London SW1P 1DQ
UK
Tel: 071 976 7611/7612
Fax: 071 976 6113

ACTION AID
Vicky Johnson — Environment Policy Analyst
Hamlyn House
Archway
London
UK
Tel: 071 281 4101
Fax: 071 272 0899

AGRO ACTION/DEUTSCHE WELTHUNGERHILFE
Margrit Rohm — Project Officer Latin America
Adenauerallee 134
G-5300 Bonn 1
Germany
Tel: 010 492 2822 880
Fax: 010 492 2822 0710

BREAD FOR THE WORLD — representing **GOOD GROUP**
Gerlind Melsbach — Women in Development Officer
Stafflenbergstrasse 76
D-7000 Stutgart 10
Germany
Tel: 010 4971 1215 9426
Fax: 010 4971 1215 9288

CAFOD — representing **EURO-CIDSE**
Catherine Morgan — Co-financing Officer
Romero Close
Stockwell Road
London SW9 9TY
UK
Tel: 071 733 7900
Fax: 071 274 9630

CHANGE
Georgina Ashworth — Director
5 Central Buildings
Rye Lane
London SE15 5DW
UK
Tel: 071 277 6187
Fax: 071 277 6187

COMMISSION OF THE EC
DG VIII — A1
Dorothée Versteylen
Rue de Geneve 12
1140 Brussels
Belgium
Tel: 010 322 299 9823
Fax: 010 322 299 2907

EUROSTEP SECRETARIAT
Brita Nielsen
115 Rue Stevin
1040 Brussels
Belgium
Tel: 010 322 231 1659
Fax: 010 322 230 3750

HELINAS
Lois Woestman
9 Orminioy Str
GR-115 28 Athens
Greece
Tel: 010 3017 234 456
Fax: 010 3017 237 662

HIVOS
Corina Straatsma — WID Co-ordinator
Raamweg 16
NL-2596 HL The Hague
The Netherlands
Tel: 010 3170 363 6907
Fax: 010 3170 361 7447

IBIS
Diana Vinding — Programme Officer responsible for Gender
Catherine Hasse — Member
Norrbrogade 68 B
DK-200 Copenhagen N
Denmark
Tel: 010 453 135 8788
Fax: 010 453 135 0696

INSTITUTE OF DEVELOPMENT STUDIES
Naila Kabeer — Fellow
University of Sussex
Brighton
BN1 9RE
UK
Tel: 0273 606261
Fax: 0273 621202

IRISH COMMISSION FOR JUSTICE AND PEACE/WIDE
Pauline Eccles — Research and Development Officer
169 Booterstown Road
Blackrock
Dublin
Ireland
Tel: 010 353 1288 4853
Fax: 010 353 1283 4161

MANI TESE
Silvia Ferrari — External Relations Officer
Nadia de Mond — Latin America Desk
Via Cavenghi, 4
I-20149 Milan
Italy
Tel: 010 392 4800 8617
Fax: 010 392 4812 296

MELLEMFOLKELIGT SAMVIRKE
Gitte Berg — Gender Consultant, General Secretariat
Ellen Farr — Section leader, Development Education and
    Information
Borgergade 10-14
DK-1300 Copenhagen K
Denmark
Tel: 010 4533 326 244
Fax: 010 4533 156 243

MOLISV
Anna Foca — Director
Josita Profeta — Project Officer Angola
Piazza Albania, 10
I-00153 Rome
Italy
Tel: 010 396 5730 0330
Fax: 010 396 5744 869

NCOS

Marianne Vergeyle — Co-ordinator Women's Desk
Ilse Uyttenhove — Women's Desk
Johan Cottenie — Head NCOS Project Service, Overseas Department,
1 Vlasfabriekstraat 11
B-1060 Brussels
Belgium
Tel: 010 322 539 2620
Fax: 010 322 539 1343

NOVIB

Miriam van Reisen — Consultant on women and human rights
Ellen Sprenger — Sectoral specialist, women/gender and
    development
Adrie Papma — Sectoral specialist, women/gender and development
Amaliastraat 7
NL-2514 JC The Hague
Netherlands
Tel: 010 3170 342 1621
Fax: 010 3170 361 4461

OIKOS

Maria Natividade Cardoso
Av. Viconde Valmor 35, 3
P-1000 Lisbon
Portugal
Tel: 010 3511 796 4719
Fax: 010 3511 793 9791

OXFAM UK/I

Eugenia Piza-López, Coordinator, Gender and Development Unit
    (GADU)
Bridget Walker, Adviser, GADU
Candida March, Coordinator, Women's Linking Project, GADU
Sue Smith, Resources Officer, GADU
Kate Allport, Selma Chalabi, Administrators, GADU
Monica Press, Regional Manager, Middle East
Audrey Bronstein, Programme Services Director
Claire Godfrey, Researcher, Public Policy Department
Mary van Lieshout, Area Campaigns Executive, Oxfam Ireland
Tina Wallace, Coordinator, Planning and Evaluation Unit

Oxfam House
274 Banbury Road
Oxford OX2 7DZ
UK
Tel: 0865 311311
Fax: 0865 312600

SCHOOL OF DEVELOPMENT STUDIES
Sarah White — Member of Faculty
University of East Anglia
Norwich
NR4 7TJ
UK
Tel: 0603 56161 x-2327
Fax: 0603 505 262

TERRE DES HOMMES
Annegret Winter-Stettin
Ruppenkampstrasse 11a
G-4500 Osnabruck
Germany
Tel: 010 495 4171 010
Fax: 010 495 4170 7233

WIDE
Helen O'Connell — UK President
Flat 2A
77 Anson Road
London N7 OAX
UK
Tel: 071 607 8390
Fax: 071 607 8390

Mandy Macdonald — Consultant editor
4 Mile End Place
Aberdeen AB2 4PZ
UK
Tel: 0422 463 6661
Fax: 0422 463 6661